Diaries from the Days of Sail

Other works by R. C. Bell

Board and Table Games of Many Civilizations, Oxford University Press, 1960.

Board and Table Games of Many Civilizations, Volume II, Oxford University Press, 1969.

Tangram Teasers, Corbitt & Hunter, 1965.

Discovering Old Board Games, Shire Press, 1973.

Commercial Coins 1787-1804, Corbitt & Hunter, 1963.

Copper Commercial Coins 1811-1819, Corbitt & Hunter, 1964.

Tradesmen's Tickets and Private Tokens 1785-1819, Corbitt & Hunter, 1966.

Specious Tokens 1784-1804, Corbitt & Hunter, 1969.

Tyneside Pottery, Studio Vista, 1971.

The Use of Skin Grafts, Oxford University Press, 1973.

Diaries
from the
Days of Sail

Edited by
R.C. Bell

Introduction by
Alan Villiers

Technical Editor C.P. Seyd

Holt, Rinehart and Winston

NEW YORK   CHICAGO   SAN FRANCISCO

Published simultaneously in Canada by Holt, Rinehart and Winston of Canada, Ltd.

Library of Congress Catalog number: 74-4411.
ISBN 0-03-012941-9

Printed and bound in Great Britain.

Produced by Carter Nash Cameron Ltd., 25 Lloyd Baker Street, London WC1.

Jacket illustration: The *Dreadnought* off Tuskar Light; lithograph by Currier, reproduced by courtesy of the National Maritime Museum, London.

The editor is greatly indebted to Mrs Marion Wood, of Vancouver, B.C., for the loan of C. H. Clarke's diary; Mrs B. Brown, of Rothbury, Northumberland, for that of Alexander Whitehead, and the painting of the *Vanguard;* and Mr Alfred Whitehead for the biography of his parents and the photographs of his father.

It is also a great pleasure to acknowledge the kindness of the Director of the Sunderland Art Gallery; the Director of the Tate Gallery; and the Trustees of the National Maritime Museum for permitting the reproduction of paintings in their care.

The editor has received invaluable help from many sources, including K. R. Mason Esq., Deputy Shipping Editor of Lloyds; L. E. Kimpton Esq., Curator of the Archives, P &. O-Orient Lines; R. Blundell Esq., Tynemouth Borough Librarian; W. Taylor Esq., Assistant Director, Shipley Art Gallery, Gateshead; M. S. Robinson Esq., Curator of Pictures, National Maritime Museum; and J. H. Wilson Esq., Chief Assistant Curator, Sunderland Art Gallery; and to all these gentlemen he is most grateful for the time and trouble they have taken in various aspects of reseach.

The editor is also deeply indebted to Charles P. Seyd Esq., the technical editor, for his assistance with nautical terms, and for translating some of the difficult passages in the diaries when the handwriting had deteriorated during stormy weather.

Contents

Foreword

These diaries describe a way of life which has passed for ever. The three writers were drawn from different social backgrounds, and their journeys contrast in purpose. C. H. Clarke was a young man of leisure making a Grand Tour, but chose to travel in North America instead of the more usual progress through the capital cities of Europe. Alexander Whitehouse was a cabin boy on the first voyage of his career as a professional sailor; while the homesick Edward Lacey faced an unknown future in the new land 'Down Under'.

Nothing has been added to these accounts, except explanatory notes: spelling mistakes and obvious errors have been corrected, and repetitions deleted; for these diaries were 'rough copies' written at odd moments on deck, in bunks, or any quiet corner available to the writers. The editor has matched the text with contemporary illustrations from the works of Bartlett, Allom, Finden and others. The atmosphere of these fine mid-nineteenth century engravings may surprise readers conditioned to photographic reproductions. Often minor features in these pictures are of major interest.

Introduction

In the days of the long-voyage sailing-ship, the idea of keeping some sort of personal record of the voyage was fairly general, though more so among passengers than seamen. The passengers had the time, not much else to notice and little else to do, and both ship and voyage could be fascinating. The men before the mast had little spare time, the life to them was commonplace and full, and a great many could not write anyway.

Here we are fortunate to have a fascinating trio of diaries, two from observant passengers, and the third from an apprentice seaman. Together they present a good cross-section of sailing merchant-ship voyaging in the mid-19th century, excellently chosen — the woman-hating Mr Clarke on a Western Ocean voyage as a passenger in the 1830s, from England to the St Lawrence; the terse young apprentice Alex Whitehead in the 626 ton China trader *Vanguard* on her maiden voyage to Hong Kong, Shanghai, and back again; another passenger who sailed in the ship *Orient* in the early 1860's from England to S Australia.

The Western Ocean 'packet' could be a very tough ship, often a tramp freighter roughly converted to transport as many unfortunate humans to the westwards as possible and let the Lord take care of them. 'The women the ugliest and most disagreeable I ever beheld,' moans diarist Clarke, a few days out in his west-bound packet: but what sort of misogynist was he? He lands in Canada, and there are fascinating glimpses of travel both in Canada and U.S.A., including a trip by 'canal packet boat hauled by three horses' — but he is quickly moaning about the women there, too. All women, apparently: but he moans also about the 'expensive' hotel at Buffalo, N.Y., where he is charged $1.50 a day, meals included.

The Orient Line passenger, Mr Lacey, is a more helpful observer, at any rate at sea. The ship *Orient* was 9 years old in 1862 when he joined her as a cabin passenger (he had a cabin aft, ate with the captain, was privileged to take his exercise walking the poop — the merchant-man's quarter-deck). The food was good for she carried a small farmyard of 49 animals including sheep, hogs, a cow and calf (the calf soon turned into veal) as well as 250 fowls. Life in the *Orient* at least for the first-class passengers was good, though in bad weather they could be 'smacked about like so many rats in a tub' and the whole poop leapt high on the crest of every sea when she was galloping in the great gales of the Roaring Forties.

Mr Lacey's was a standard Australian passage — the fight out of the English Channels, the romp through the Trades, the dribble in the Doldrums, then the headlong, wet and windy rush down south in the Roaring Forties towards Port Adelaide. Thirty years later, that extraordinary seaman J. Conrad was Mate of the ship *Torrens*, one of the last successors of the *Orient* in that trade. But she had few passengers by that time.

The *Orient* took 82 days, though she had done it in 75. (We did it in 70 in 1922 in the *Lawhill* with a crew of about twenty and no passengers at all: the *Lawhill* was over 3000 tons, a big workhorse of a four-masted barque.)

Apprentice Whitehead offsets Passenger Lacey very well, and supplements him too. Whitehead is 17 years old. He paints deadeyes, helps set studding-sails, scrapes the poop-deck, helps serve the t'gall'nt and royal footropes *aloft,* he says, though this was too dangerous for his successors ever to do. (We sent those high footropes down on deck where they could be thoroughly examined and cared for in safety.) On another day he is 'down in the f'o'c's'l helping the Old Man,' or 'preparing the guns against pirates' in the China Sea. (The 'Old Man' is the master: what was he doing in the forecastle, the abode of the sailors?) Our apprentice is brief and to the point, never moved by anything or to any reflections.

'Took in the studding-sails: put the cables (anchor) below: the cook killed a sheep' — that is the entry for one day, but that was a lot of heavy work for everybody. The studding-sails were extra sails boomed out beyond the yards, set awkwardly in fine weather almost doubling the ship's square canvas (and trebling the work). Cables by that era were heavy iron chain, tarry, slimey from the bottom of the sea, and they had to be man-handled into tractable and perfect stow down in the dark and airless bowels of the chain-locker in the ship's eyes. Killing a sheep was a messy, laborious business.

But the deepwater square-rigged ship's days were always overfull of hard labour and Alex Whitehead paid no heed to doing his share of it. In port the same, except that the work of ship-care and ship-cleaning is now increased by cargo-handling, also done by the crew. Alex finds himself helping to load 'a lot of wood that had a funny stink': maybe some opium too, for while she waits her cargo of new season's teas to rush off to London, the ship fills in time and earns good money by turning into local freighter on the China Coast. Then jam-packed with fragrant tea, she is off on the tremendous haul to London — 15,000 miles of it! She makes it in 103 days, clipper time. Our apprentice takes that in his stride too. The voyage ends: so does his journal.

These three diaries are of the fascinating stuff of sea history in the days of Sail. What ships they were, and what sailors! *All* their long voyages were memorable and in their triumph over circumstance could be inspiring, for Man may know no more harmonious, soul-satisfying progress than the softly silent passage of the working sailing-ship through those glorious agents of the Creator the great Trade Winds, under skilful, patient, quietly expert seamen in control of the beautiful, silent and effective creation of masts, cordage, canvas, yards that was the square-rigged ship — that glorious triumph of long-continued effort, a contribution to his work of infinite worth, now thrown away!

It is of value to preserve these simple accounts come down to us by chance from these widely different diarists. One of these days, survivors among our brothers might have to try to grope their way back to these skills again — if some man-made holocaust has not by then destroyed also the sea wind.

Alan Villiers

A page from Edward Lacey's diary.

To the memory of A. Basil Lubbock
who did so much to preserve for posterity knowledge
of the last days of sail.

References

Allom, T. & Wright, G. N.   *China*, Vols 1–4, London, 1843.

Bartlett, W. H. & Willis, N. P.   *American Scenery*, Vols 1–2, London, *c*1840.

Bartlett, W. H. & Willis, N. P.   *Canadian Scenery*, Vols 1–2, London, 1842.

Finden, E. *Ports, Harbours & Watering Places of Great Britain*, London, *c*1838.

Lloyd's Registry of Shipping (various years).

Lubbock, A. B.   *The China Clippers*, 7th edition, 1929.

Lubbock, A. B.   *The Colonial Clippers*, Glasgow, 1921.

Lubbock, A. B.   *The Last of the Windjammers*, Vol 1, pages 45–8, reprinted 1963.

American Journey

1834

C.H. Clarke

The first of these diaries was written in 1834 by the editor's great great grandfather, C. H. Clarke Esq., of Bilston, Staffordshire. The original manuscript was destroyed many years ago by a great uncle, but fortunately a copy had been made and the present account is taken from this through the courtesy of Mrs Marion Wood, of Vancouver, British Columbia. The first few pages are missing, and the account starts in mid Atlantic, on board the ship Caroline, *bound from England to Montreal. Details of sailings of the* Caroline *and the* Orpheus *are given in Appendix B.*

The ship Helvellyn, *built in 1826: the* Caroline, *on which C. H. Clarke was a passenger, was a similar vessel. From a painting by Walters.*

Monday April 14, 1834. Longitude 41° 22'. A great many porpoises playing about the vessel, some are very large and from twenty to thirty feet in length.

Tuesday April 15. Longitude 42°. Blew very hard during the night, and the sea is running high. We are now hove to, with the helm lashed. The sea being so rough it is very awkward at meal times, with a good chance of losing your grub, or of having someone else's in your lap.

Wednesday April 16. The wind is again in our favour, but the sea has not subsided from the contrary winds and we are only making about six knots. The barometer is going up, though it is still excessively low. *2 p.m.* A storm came out of the NNE, the wind is very strong and we are obliged to reef in all sail and heave to. The sea is running higher than I have ever seen before.

Thursday April 17. Latitude 43° 38'. Longitude 42° 41'. The wind blew very hard during the fore part of the night, and many passengers were up on account of fright, but it abated a little towards morning. Wind NNW and we are making about 2½ knots, but are going too far south.

Friday April 18. Longitude 46°. All in high spirits as the wind has changed in our favour and is SSW. We are going at the famous rate of 10 knots. Three sails in sight but at a great distance. This morning we broke the fore topsail yard, but soon remedied it by putting up another.

Saturday April 19. Latitude 44°. Longitude 47° 48′ 15″. We expected to be on the Banks of Newfoundland this morning, but unfortunately the wind changed and is now nearly dead ahead. The people on board are getting their fishing tackle ready to catch cod. I suppose we are in the most perilous part of our voyage owing to ice at this time of the year. Many sea-hogs appeared this morning. They are a species of porpoise, but leap several feet into the air, whereas the porpoise merely shows himself at the top of the water, and the latter are also much larger. The weather is colder this morning and foggy. This is usual on the Banks, which extend about a hundred and sixty miles. I suppose we may expect to be colder yet.

Sunday April 20. Longitude 50°. A most uncomfortable day, with the wind blowing very strongly from the NE, accompanied by heavy rain. We are on the Banks, and sometimes reaching 10 knots. This morning we shipped the most sea yet, and the decks were so wet and slippery that it was impossible to stand on them. I think it has been the most uncomfortable day of my life. About eight o'clock this morning a very large iceberg appeared three to four miles to leeward, like a white cloud rising from the sea. We shall be across the principal bank by night if the wind continues. It is bitterly cold, although the thermometer is still 1° above zero. There are many birds flying around the vessel, and a brig is in sight. Yesterday we saw several vessels. At four p.m. we sounded sandy bottom in 37 fathoms of water. Still raining.

Monday April 21. The rigging is completely covered with ice and it is very foggy and cold. We have just hailed a small brig from Greenock bound for Newfoundland. They started on the 23rd, two days before us, and have seen great quantities of ice. They differ from us in their calculations, being about two degrees behind us in their longitude. We are going about $3\frac{1}{2}$ knots, and if we become becalmed may have some sport catching codfish.

Tuesday April 22. A fine clear morning with the wind direct ahead. We have passed over the principal bank and are in deep water again, and from the cold expect to be stopped by ice off the Gulf of Cape Ray, where the *Caroline* has been detained for a week or more for the last two seasons. The thermometer is 45°F in the cabin and 33°F on deck. An Irish schooner has just hailed us and wanted to know the latitude and longitude. Many small birds called divers are around our ship.

Wednesday April 23. Longitude 53° 44′. The weather is fine and clear, but very cold. It blew tremendously all night, and I am beginning to wish we were safely in port.

Thursday April 24. Longitude 53° 30′. It is now quite calm. There is too much sameness on a ship which is irksome to those without employment, though probably very different for those with work to do. It is 38°F in the cabin, and 31°F at 7 a.m. this morning on deck.

Friday April 25. The wind was favourable for a few hours during the night but it is now calm and snowing fast. The barometer is very low. We are about 250 miles from Cape Ray*. I fear my log will not be very entertaining for there is a scarcity of interesting subjects. In all my life I never saw such a quarrelsome set of people as there are on board, while the women are the ugliest and most disagreeable I ever beheld; it will be as great a treat to see a decent good-looking girl again as *terra-firma* itself!

Saturday April 26. Latitude 44° 18'. Longitude 55° 17'. Still a head wind and we have only made six degrees in a week. We are now over one of the smaller banks called the Green Bank in twenty-five fathoms of water.

Sunday April 27. Longitude 56°. There was a heavy fall of snow during the night which lay two feet deep on the deck. This morning a grampus or a small whale was seen spouting up water, but we were not near enough to be sure which. During the night we lost one of our passengers from a brain fever, and tossed him over this morning with a bag of sand tied to his feet. Not a pleasant idea! It is a beautiful clear day but very cold. The wind is nearly west and more in our favour.

Monday April 28. We had a nice breeze during the night and made about 8 knots, but it seems there will soon be another fall of snow as we can hardly see two yards ahead, making it rather dangerous. *11 a.m.* We think we are now close to Cape Ray, and sailing about 9 knots. The snow is falling fast. *12 noon.* We have just passed a large ice field extending many miles. In one part there was an opening through which we passed, the ice in places being nine feet thick. *6 p.m.* Cape Ray is now in sight. It is about three weeks since we last saw land, but this is rather dreary, being nearly covered with snow. Never was there a better seaman than our captain who was not a mile out in his calculations when we made land. The wind is now directly ahead, blowing out of the Gulf.

Wednesday April 30. The wind is still unfavourable, but it is a beautiful clear day, with St Paul Island and Cape Breton on our larboard†, and Cape Ray to starboard. The land is covered with snow, and the coast is considered dangerous. There is ice in sight, and a vessel has just passed through it. We can see some eight vessels in all. *2 p.m.* It is quite calm with the sea as smooth as possible. There are many birds around us; geese, ducks, and divers, and every now and then a seal appears.

*The south-western tip of Newfoundland.
†Larboard (now port): left; starboard: right.

MAY

Thursday May 1.   We have been moving nicely during the night with the wind in the north-east, and soon should see Anticosti.

Friday May 2.   Almost a calm yet we have been making 2 to 3 knots with a south-westerly wind, and passing Anticosti island with the sea as smooth as a pond. Lower Canada is in sight and appears to be covered with snow.

Yesterday we had an auction sale of the effects of the late James Reed, who died of typhus fever, though this was not known at the time by most of the passengers.

Saturday May 3.   Last night we had a dance. We are now becalmed. I saw several whales this morning.

Sunday May 4.   Last night the pilot came aboard. He earns about fourteen guineas for taking us up to Quebec, and navigating the river is very dangerous on account of the fogs. The Thickshaw mountains* are in view although we are about 160 miles away. At first they appeared like clouds. The river is now about 60 miles wide.

Monday May 5.   We are now experiencing the mischief of fog and nearly ran on shore in a bay; the vessel is being towed out by boat, but if it had happened at night it might have been very awkward. There is scarcely a breath of wind, yet twenty-four hours good blow would take us to Quebec which is less than 200 miles away. Our best day's run in the Atlantic was 270 miles in the twenty-four hours.

Tuesday May 6.   We made about 80 miles during the night. Yesterday we had a treat on board with plenty of wine and liquor, but soda-water was in great request this morning! Numerous vessels are in sight sailing to Quebec.

Wednesday May 7.   The wind is from the west and we make slow progress. There are many seals but they keep their distance. A white porpoise appeared today which is not unusual in this part of the world. *6 p.m.* The wind has changed to the east with heavy rain. In the New World it appears that easterly winds bring rain, while westerly or south-westerly winds from over the large land tracts bring fine weather.

Thursday May 8.   We were obliged to anchor during the night as the wind dropped and the current ran so strongly against us that it was impossible to make headway. *10 a.m.* The wind is directly ahead from the south-west and we are lying at anchor about 100 miles from Quebec. The river is about seven miles wide, and to larboard is a very picturesque Canadian village. The houses are made of wood, being what they term log-houses.

Friday May 9.   Last night about 10 o'clock the wind dropped and

*Probably the Shickshock mountains.

Georgetown, a Canadian village.

we got under weigh as the tide was in our favour, but we were obliged to cast anchor again this morning. All the way up the river the views are very fine, and it is a most splendid river with numerous whales, seals and white porpoises.

Saturday May 10. We cast anchor again at eleven o'clock last night, but got under weigh about 2 a.m. to take advantage of the tide which runs very rapidly at about 6 knots. I believe it never runs more than $3\frac{1}{2}$ knots in the Thames. The river is the most dangerous part of our voyage. We have already passed two wrecked vessels, one three days ago, and the other this morning called the *Cherub* from Greenock. It is jammed in amongst the rocks, and was wrecked on one of the dark nights at the beginning of the week, probably on Tuesday. The winds in the river are particularly changeable. You may see at the same moment one vessel carrying along on a fair wind, another becalmed and a third with it directly ahead; this is caused by the high mountains on each side. There are also many small islands, some are nothing more than rocks, others are covered with brushwood. We passed one yesterday called Hare Island with numerous hares upon it from which it derives its name. All the way on our larboard side are houses, but to starboard are very high hills with their summits covered with snow.

Sunday May 11. Yesterday at 3 p.m. we reached Grosse Island, the quarantine ground which is about 30 miles from Quebec. There are many vessels here, and numerous others in view coming up the river. This morning we landed all our passengers, other than cabin passengers, with their bedding and dirty linen to get them aired and cleaned. Two of our passengers' beds were hove overboard on account of their filthy condition.

1 p.m. Our captain kindly let the remainder of us go on the island; a great treat after being cooped up in the vessel for nearly seven weeks, and we ran about the island like wild beings; it is very rocky and nearly covered with trees. There are no inhabitants except for the persons appointed for the quarantine. We bought plenty of bread and fresh butter for the last night which was the greatest treat imaginable after being so long without it.

Two steamboats came down as far as the island today from Quebec with passengers upon pleasure. They appear much finer than ours, being more handsomely fitted up and burn wood instead of coal.

A vessel alongside from Ireland has about 400 people on board. They lost nineteen on the voyage, and as there are as many ill at the moment they are likely to be detained for some time. There is a telegraph on the island, so that Quebec is informed of vessels within five minutes of their arrival.

Monday May 12. Last night we anchored about four miles from

Below: *Quebec from the opposite shore of the St Lawrence.* Above right: *Prescott Gate, Quebec.* Right: *the Market Place, Quebec.*

Quebec, after nearly running down a small schooner in the darkness. *10 a.m.* Just passed the Falls of Montmorency. *11 p.m.* When we reached Quebec a party of several passengers walked through the town and of all the places that ever I saw, this beats all. It is a most miserable place. The day was very wet, which perhaps made it appear worse than it really is. The cattle are very small, but the horses

though also small are excellent. It requires a good lookout to prevent being taken in. Most of the inhabitants speak French well, and the town is very much like those in France. We gave a dinner to our worthy captain on board the *Caroline,* and kept it up 'till morning. *Tuesday May 13. 7 p.m.* Now on board the steam vessel *Canada.* She came alongside to take us and our luggage; and also took many passengers from another vessel, principally Irish, and a very pretty sample they were of the land of cakes! This morning I went with others to see the Heights of Abraham, and the monument to General

Wolfe. The town is well fortified from the heights. There is a peculiar craft for conveyance across the river, propelled by horses going round and with paddle wheels similar to our steamboats. They also have a most annoying number of different coins. A stranger now on board says he was twelve months before he became acquainted with them all.

Lord and Lady Aylmea, and the Archdeacon of Quebec with his son, and several officers who are excellent fellows, are now on board. *Wednesday May 14.* It snowed hard all night and continues to do so. We landed the Governor and his suite at Sorel, where he has a country residence, and as we were detained about an hour, most of us went on shore for a stroll. The weather cleared a little and it was very pleasant. We took on board a quantity of wood for firing. There is a vessel in tow which retards our progress. The *Canada* is a fine steamer; 180 horse power, and fitted up in first rate style. I never saw anything to equal it. We have also the best of living. The fare to Montreal, 180 miles from Quebec, is six dollars with board included. There are many steamers on the river, and they appear far superior to ours in England. Most of them are low pressure, with the beam above the deck.

Thursday May 15. We arrived at Montreal about 10 p.m. and some of us went on shore, but from the darkness of the night were soon

Left: *Quebec, the town and the waterfront.* Below left: *a view from Quebec citadel.* Below: *the citadel.*

glad to return. Our passengers are very busy getting their luggage on shore; some have several tons. Montreal is far preferable to Quebec; there is a fine brick Market House newly erected, and a handsome Catholic cathedral. The scenery from the heights is very imposing. Living expenses are moderate, board, etc., being three fourths of a dollar per day. A party of us hired a boat for two dollars each, the first nine miles being by canal to Lachine.

Friday May 16. We stayed on board the boat during the night but had no sleep and started at 4 a.m. Three of us tired of this way of

Above left: *shipping passing a light tower near Coburg.* Left: *Montreal from the river.* Above: *the cathedral and waterfront, Montreal.*

travel and landed at Lachine, a pretty little village where we break-fasted and then took steamer to the Cascades about twenty-four miles from Lachine. The country appears very productive although stony, and the stones are of enormous size. Wheat of sixty-two pounds sells at five shillings to five and threepence per bushel. The inhabitants are a mixture of French, English, Irish and Canadians.

A map of Upper Canada in 1842.

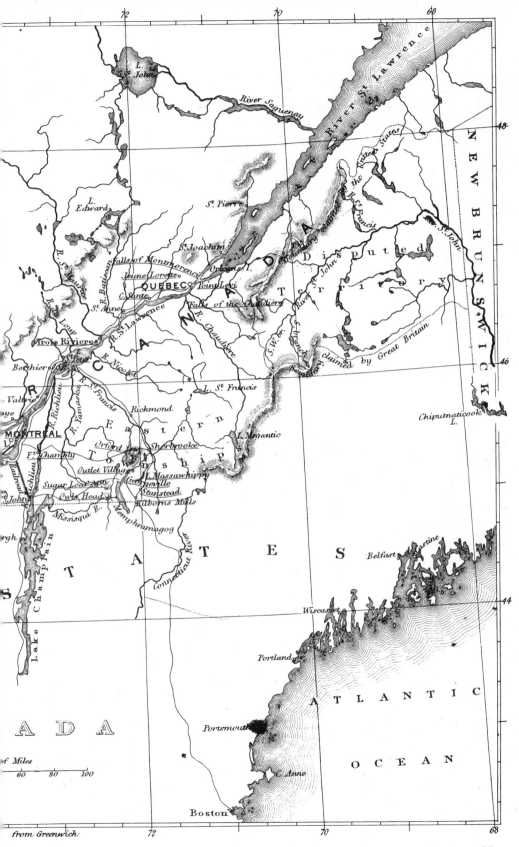

We took coach at the Cascades and arrived at Coteau du Lac at 7 p.m. The roads are the worst I ever witnessed, and as the coach was full I had to sit on the roof. It was the greatest difficulty in the world to keep there! The horses were excellent. Coteau du Lac is sixteen miles from Cascades, and on leaving the coach we boarded the *Neptune,* a steamer of ninety horse power.

Montreal from the mountain. Below: *the St Lawrence near Montreal.*

Saturday May 17. We arrived early in the morning at Cornwall, which is forty-four miles from Coteau du Lac, and then had to rise at five a.m. to take coach again as rapids prevent the river being navigable. The roads were worse than before and an English coach would not go fifty yards without breaking down. After twelve miles we took to steaming it again. *7 a.m.* Left on board the *Brockville*, steamboat. We touched at Prescott, a considerable town, and then onward to Brockville, a pretty village in the English style. We waited there about two

Above: *Prescott from Ogdensburgh Harbour.*
Below: *Brockville.*

hours for another steamer and went on shore and enjoyed ourselves. During the day we passed through many rapids and against a very strong current. There are numerous small islands in the river which are delightful and some of our passengers who have travelled a great deal say nothing equals the scenery of the St Lawrence. We have reached Dickenous Landing Place, which is fifty miles from Brockville.

Sunday May 18. Last night about 8 p.m. boarded the *William IV*, steamer of a hundred horse power with only one engine, to take us

to Toronto, late York, about 250 miles from Brockville. Arrived at Kingston at the entrance to Lake Ontario at 10 a.m., and went to church; quite a treat not having been inside one for the last eight weeks.

Kingston is an extensive, well-fortified town with many genteel houses. The soldiers appear to be healthy and well dressed and have

Left: *rapids on the St Lawrence.* Below left: *among the Thousand Islands.* Below: *Kingston.* Bottom: *view from Kingston citadel.*

a better appearance than our troops at home. A wooden bridge some half-mile long extends from the town across part of the river.

We took on more passengers and a quantity of luggage. The cabin is now full. We left Kingston at 7.30 p.m. The remarkable plainness of the ladies we have had on our travels, not only from London to Quebec but all the way up the river, is really astonishing.

Monday May 19. Lake Ontario is so vast that you may fancy yourself on the Atlantic. Last night we were entirely out of sight of land, and the colour of the water is nearly that of the sea; I think from its great depth. *8 a.m.* Now stopping at Coburg to take in more fuel and passengers. A few years ago there were only a few houses, and now it contains 1,500 inhabitants. *9 a.m.* Touched at Port Hope. *4 p.m.* Arrived at Toronto: about 5,000 miles from home, and 75 from every other place! It is a large town, but very full and we had

Above left: *Kingston citadel*. Left: *Coburg*. Top: *Port Hope*. Above: *the landing stage at Toronto*.

great difficulty in finding lodging; eventually we were accommodated at the Steam Boat Hotel, kept by a Yankee. My bed was in a kind of lobby with a continual thoroughfare, but being the first night on shore for more than eight weeks I slept soundly.

FARES

Six dollars, board included	180 miles Quebec to Montreal ...		Steam
Eight dollars, and find for our-selves	9 miles to Lachine		Durham Boat
	24 ,, ,, Cascades		Steam
	16 ,, ,, Coteau du Lac ...		Coach
	44 ,, ,, Cornwall		Steam
	12 ,, ,, Dickenous Landing		Coach
	38 ,, ,, Prescott		Steam
	12 ,, ,, Brockville		Steam
Eight dollars, board included	10 ,, ,, Kingston		Steam
	110 ,, ,, Coburg		Steam
	10 ,, ,, Port Hope		Steam
	60 ,, ,, Toronto		Steam
	345		

Tuesday May 20. They keep a very good table at our hotel at a cost of six dollars a week. Living expenses are lower than in England, the price of the best brandy is ten shillings per gallon, and other liquors at the same rate.

There are several Yankees at our table, and it is curious that before we have half done our dinner they are off with their food in their mouths, not giving themselves time to swallow it. As it was a lovely day three of us started off into the woods on a shooting excursion and enjoyed it amazingly; had plenty of sport and managed to kill a quail and sundry small birds, with some squirrels. The woods are beautiful, the pines being particularly lofty and some are of immense size.

Wednesday May 21. We are waiting for our luggage which has not yet arrived. Toronto is very lately incorporated; no doubt some day it will be an extensive place. Took a stroll through the town and went into a fine windmill on the outskirts. Sir John Colburn, the Governor, has a very good house at the west end, not far from Parliament House.

Friday May 23. We walked along the banks of the river Humber for several miles, and nearly lost ourselves in the woods; were be-nighted and had to walk almost ten miles after sunset; arrived home at 11 o'clock and very tired. There were a great variety of small birds, including a very beautiful little one called the red-bird, and another about the same size, known as the blue-bird. The blue jay is also very pretty, while some of the numerous woodpeckers of which there are about six varieties are very handsome. There were plenty of bull frogs, sounding like old men with bad coughs.

Saturday May 24. We took boat and went after duck, which are in great abundance, but only killed a couple as they are very shy and difficult to approach.

Indian tents in a forest.

Sunday May 25. Went to church, a fine building, and well filled with a most respectable congregation. Some of the girls were very good looking!

Monday May 26. Again went out shooting on the water. There were plenty of ducks but they took good care we should not get near them.

Tuesday May 27. Again shooting in the boat, up a small river called the Don. There were many tortoises on the banks, and we killed several. The temperature rose to 86°F in the shade.

Wednesday May 28. Some of our party who stayed in the Durham boat arrived about midnight in the *United States,* a huge Yankee steamer with an almighty cargo of passengers – nearly 600! Most landed at Toronto and it was fascinating to witness the scene. The captain wanted to leave in three hours, and made them land with their considerable luggage at once. I never saw such confusion, and through all the noise and bustle many half naked women and children were asleep on the deck. I was at work until all our party's luggage was on shore.

Thursday May 29. We are on board the *United Kingdom,* a high pressure, ninety horse power steamer bound for Queenston forty miles from Toronto and seven from Niagara Falls, fare $2.50. Last night there was a fall of rain, otherwise the weather has been very fine all the time we were at Toronto, and excessively hot. The other day I turned up my shirt sleeves while rowing, and now my arms are so painful that I am obliged to sling them up: they are so swollen that

Below: *Toronto fish market.* Above right: *Queenston and General Brock's monument.* Right: *the Niagara river below the falls.*

I cannot wear my coat. Sometimes the temperature in summer reaches 107°F in the shade, and much higher in the sun. By the time summer is over we shall be melted away and nothing left but skin and bones! *Friday May 30.*   Queenston is a small village on the banks of the river Niagara seven miles from its mouth. We slept at the Yankee

Inn and had a good bed and breakfast for 50 cents each. On the heights is a monument to General Brock who was killed there in a battle with the Yankees in 1812, when 200 English troops defeated 2,000 Americans; killed many and took the remainder prisoners. The monument is 120 ft. high.

We walked with our guns from the town of Niagara along the banks of the river to the Falls, and saw several black squirrels about the size of a small cat with a long bushy tail. We killed a partridge about the size of an English pheasant, and dined at a village called Drummonville. The Falls are beyond description. The spray rises in

Niagara Falls; above left: *Horseshoe Falls and observation tower.* Left: *Goat Island.* Above: *Table Rock.*

clouds above the highest trees on Goat Island which is above the Falls and separates it into two halves. The sun shining on the spray is very beautiful and appears like a rainbow, and the moon gives the

Landing on the American side of Niagara Falls. Right: *travelling by stage: a Canadian coach passing through a village.*

same appearance. I am told that the noise of the falling water can be heard for forty miles. The Pavilion Hotel near the Falls reminds me of the Star and Garter at Richmond and is a fine establishment.

Saturday May 31.   The Horse Shoe Falls are magnificent; a hundred and fifty-eight feet high, and six hundred and thirty yards across. The American Falls are nearly in a straight line, and a hundred and sixty-four feet high and three hundred yards wide. Table Rock projects over fifty feet, and it appears as though it will soon fall as there is a large crack about thirty feet from the edge.

We took a boat over to Manchester, a small American town which communicates by a bridge with Goat Island, and close to the Horse Shoe Falls is an observatory with a fine view of the immense body of falling water, and the stream beneath is a hundred and seventy feet deep. I bought a specimen of Indian workmanship at a small island between Goat Island and Manchester to show when home, and I also picked up a piece of rock within a yard of the Horse Shoe Falls where some men were cutting a way through the solid rock.

Today the sport was very good; killed several pigeons, some on Goat Island and some in the woods outside Manchester. I walked over to Chippawa, a small village about two and a half miles from the Falls to enquire about the steamboats. Took a walk to the Falls after dark. They were magnificent, with the flying spray appearing like sparks of fire.

JUNE

Sunday June 1. A beautiful morning and visited the Falls again, and then walked nearly a mile above the falls to a Burning Spring which was well worth seeing. The water kept boiling up and a piece of lighted paper thrown onto its surface burnt with bright yellow and blue flames. The water was dark and had a disagreeable smell. The little girl who led the way placed a wooden tube in the spring and the gas rose to the top of the tube. A piece of lighted paper held over it flashed up like our gas lights in London.

In the afternoon we took stage for Queenston, and then set out on foot about 7 p.m. for Hamilton which is about fifty miles distant. We walked eight miles to Ten Mile Creek, a small village, and as it was late all the folks had gone to bed. We called up the landlord of a small inn who found us beds.

Monday June 2. The weather has changed, yesterday it was very hot, and today one can scarcely keep warm by walking fast. We passed through St Catherine's, a large town about ten miles from Queenston, and managed to reach Beamsville, a small village where we turned in for the night. I like the countryside very much, most of the land is cultivated and the wheat is looking well.

We had good sport in the woods; putting up nine woodcocks in a small copse and managed to kill two, also a couple of quail and woodpigeons out of number. Anyone who is a good shot might live here by his gun alone, the woods are literally covered with wood-pigeons.

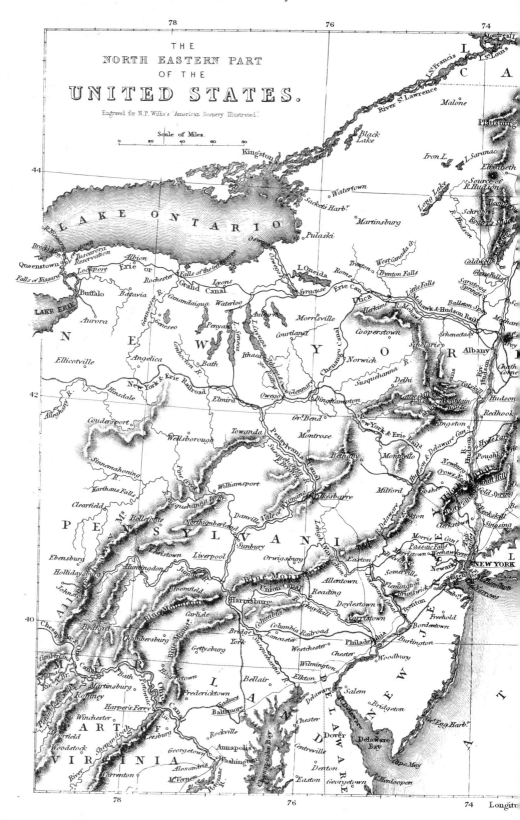

PART OF
VIRGINIA AND MARYLAND
on the same Scale

Tuesday June 3. We did not make much progress today. At Forty Mile Creek we scraped acquaintance with an Irish gentleman whose cousin in London was known to one of our party. We soon became acquainted with two other gentlemen, one of whom invited us to his house, and wished us to dine with him and stay the night. He was a miller in a large way of business with a very nice house, but as we wanted to get to Hamilton, we could not comply; but went on about two miles to a small village where one of our party was taken ill and we were obliged to stay and put him to bed. He recovered in the evening and we took coach and arrived at Hamilton some sixteen miles away at 10 p.m. and spent the night at Burley's Hotel.

Wednesday June 4. Hamilton is a sizeable town about a mile from Burlington Bay from which there is a communication to Lake Ontario. The land is very good, and the further west the better it is, but the roads are bad.

Walked to Dundas, a small town five miles from Hamilton. The land along the road was well cultivated and of the best quality I have yet seen. The price of wheat in Dundas is low; the highest quoted in the paper was three shillings and sevenpence per bushel, and flour was seventeen shillings and sixpence per barrel. I dined at Dundas and then walked back to Hamilton.

Wages are high. Today I met a lad of sixteen who had just taken a situation as a woodcutter at ten dollars a month with board and lodging, and even then he did not appear satisfied. He has two hundred acres of his own in the London district; half he has paid for out of his savings and he is now laying by to pay for the other hundred acres.

Thursday June 5. Walked seven miles with our guns to Ancaster, a nice little place where we dined and then returned to Hamilton. Killed two large squirrels, one was perfectly black and the other a dark grey: they are considered a dainty dish.

Land here is rather high. Today we were offered a site two miles the other side of Ancaster of a hundred and fifty acres, ninety being cleared, with house and buildings for $2,400.

Saturday June 7. Toronto. The weather being very hot we took it leisurely. Agues are rather prevalent here. There are some very nice houses in the city, particularly at the west end.

Sunday June 8. Went to church.

Monday June 9. After breakfast we took a boat and our guns for a long trip up the Humber river but very little sport. We saw some ducks and woodcocks but they were too wide awake for us; nevertheless as the weather was fair we had a pleasant day and the scenery was very fine. We took provisions with us and returned about 9 p.m. very tired with pulling.

Tuesday June 10. Spent the day strolling about the town.

A settler's cabin.

Wednesday June 11. My two friends with whom I have been travelling have left to go to Lake Simcoe, while I hope to pay the Yankees a visit. I expect to meet one of them again in New York and return together to England, but the other intends to settle here.

Thursday June 12. Left Toronto without much regret. The town is well laid out, but the pavements and roads are wretched, and in spite of its 10,000 population it is a very dull place. Packed up my baggage and at 7 a.m. started by the *Canada* steamer bound for Niagara where we arrived at noon, and then on by stage to Buffalo in the States. The roads were very dusty and the banks of the river from Queenston to the Falls were very high. At the Falls I took a farewell glance, and then we passed on through Chippewa to Waterloo village where we waited half an hour for the Horse Ferry to take us over to Black Rock directly opposite.

At Black Rock·the custom house officer appeared but gave me little trouble and merely looked inside my box. Then on to Buffalo by stage which set me down at 7 p.m. at the Eagle Hotel, where I stopped for the night having travelled eighty miles: – viz. forty from Toronto to Niagara, and about the same to Buffalo.

Friday June 13. Buffalo is a very impressive and busy city of 11,000 people standing on the eastern extremity of Lake Erie, which is connected with Lake Ontario by the Niagara river. There are some dozen large steamers lying in the creek, besides other vessels. Most of the houses are built of wood, but there are some fine brick ones, four or five stories high. The principal street is very long and of good width, paved on each side with brick for foot passengers. There is not a single pawnbroker here or at Toronto, which must be rather awkward for those who have been accustomed to see their uncle several times a week!

My hotel is remarkably fine with accommodation for a hundred and fifty guests, and it is often full. We have the best of everything, and so we ought for the charges are high: a dollar and a half a day, which I do not like, much as I like their comfort, for it does not agree with my pocket; and I think I shall make my exit tomorrow and proceed to Rochester by the Erie Canal which starts here and goes all the way to Albany, a distance of 363 miles, where it enters the Hudson river.

In the afternoon I took a walk to an Indian village about three miles away, where the Indians have a large extent of land, some being cultivated. I called at an Indian tavern out of curiosity and had a glass of superior ale for three cents.

The Indian ladies or squaws wear a peculiar dress of a kind of white blanket which nearly covers an under frock and beneath this are trousers, ornamented at the bottom with beads. At first glance one would take them to be men, especially when wearing their hats which closely resemble those worn by their husbands. They are not handsome, indeed I call them ugly, especially those who are not youthful. The younger ones have fine sparkling eyes, as black as jet, and very fine teeth. I have only seen one that was good looking. Their mouths are too large and their cheekbones too high for my idea of beauty, but beauty is a matter of taste. The Chinese like flat noses and pinched up feet!

The men according to my humble opinion are much the better looking; some are very tall and well made with remarkably fine expressive eyes. Their outer dress is likewise a blanket cut something to the shape of a coat. One that I met was remarkably tall with a scarlet belt of silk ornamented with beads around his waist outside his coat. Most of them understood English.

I am thinking of turning my face homewards, though it will be some time before I get there. Tomorrow on to Rochester and stay a few days; then to Albany and New York; visit Washington, Philadelphia and a few other places; and in about six weeks' time I will cross the Atlantic again, but not by way of Quebec for I had enough of that coming over; it is a much longer and more dangerous passage. By the time I reach home I will have travelled upwards of 11,000 miles.

The Erie Canal at Lockport.

I have not seen enough of Brother Jonathan* yet to form an opinion of him, but from what I have already seen, I think we shall not be in love with each other.

Saturday June 14. Travelling by canal packet boat: very pleasant in the daytime but tiring after several days and nights. There are many bridges crossing the canal which are a great bore; if you do not keep a weather eye open when standing on deck there is a chance of being knocked head over heels; I have been on my knees more times today than in the last twelvemonth! The boat is drawn by three horses at six miles an hour, and the fare to Rochester, a distance of 95 miles, including meals is $3.75. The Erie Canal is a wonderful undertaking, 363 miles in length. Lake Erie is 565 feet above the level of the Hudson river at Albany, and there are 84 locks with a rise and fall of 698 feet. The canal is forty feet wide at the surface of the water, and twenty-eight feet at the bottom, depth four feet. Between Buffalo and Lockport the canal is cut through solid rock, at a cost if I am rightly informed of a million dollars. During the day we passed several small towns and villages.

Sunday June 15. Passed an uncomfortable night without much sleep; beds were made up for us on the wooden seats about eighteen inches wide which ran round the cabin, and on these we lay stretched out

*Brother Jonathan: this expression is said to have been applied to Jonathan Turnbull, Governor of Connecticut, by George Washington; hence the term was used for a New Englander, and later became a generic name for the people of the United States, also for a representative United States citizen.

Night travel on the Erie Canal near Little Falls. Right: *the Genesee Falls, Rochester.*

like so many mackerel, while above were two rows of berths. Every now and then something touched my feet, and when I came to examine the matter I found that I was sleeping with my feet next to a lady's, and as she was rather restless, every now and then she made me the same, but I bore it with Christian-like patience. I arose early and found we were very near our port of Rochester, arriving at 5 a.m.; took my luggage and set off for the Eagle Tavern, where I am now staying.

Went to church three times today to make up for past deficiencies. There are five or six churches, and in the morning went to St Luke's, the Episcopal church; in the afternoon to a Presbyterian; and in the evening to another, ditto. The morning sermon was excellent and a very respectable congregation. The young ladies in Rochester, though modest and sedate are on the whole remarkably plain. They appear to be in poor health; are inclined to stoop; are thin, and very bad walkers, while their heels are the worst I have ever seen. They wear long clothes to hide them, but I always suspect long petticoats! Many even wear trousers! Perhaps I form too hasty an opinion, but the Yankee ladies I have seen do not appear animated, and none come up to our English Beauties.

Monday June 16. Rochester is a flourishing city of 13,000, with many store shops and an abundance of milliners and dressmakers. The Genesee river runs through the town, with mills and factories of all descriptions on its banks; a flour mill I went into had ten pairs of

stones, each pair grinding ten bushels an hour, with a total output of
seven hundred barrels of flour a day. The power came from a fall of
sixteen feet, and some three hundred yards down the river is another
fall of sixty feet. The river is about a hundred yards wide. The town
with seventy acres of stores is only in its infancy, and the oldest
person alive who was born here is not more than twenty.

I walked two miles down the stream to Carthage, a small village
where there is another fall called the Carthage Falls; indeed the river
is a series of falls between rocky banks covered with high trees. The
scenery is very beautiful.

Tuesday June 17.   Started at 5 a.m. by packet boat to Utica, a hundred and sixty miles away. The Erie Canal crosses the Genesee river
on an aqueduct a hundred yards long with a footpath on either side.
Although travelling by stage gives a better view of the country I was
glad I chose the boat for it was a wet day. We changed horses* about
every ten miles, and it seemed hard work for them. I am surprised
that the bridges across the canal were not made two or three feet
higher; several people have been killed by being knocked down; and
when on deck one must continually look ahead to stoop in time, as
the bridges are very numerous.

Wednesday June 18.   There is a hard, almost black stone in these
parts which the inhabitants call gypsum, and which they grind and
use for manure on the land. There is also plenty of Plaster of Paris
around.

We passed several small towns and villages; Port Byron, Jordan,
Canton, Syracuse, New London, Rome, etc., and arrived at Utica at
6 p.m. The fare from Rochester, board included, was $6.50.

*The horses were used to pull the boat.

Top: *Utica*. Above: *the railroad to Utica*. Right: *Albany*.

Thursday June 19. Another rainy day. Utica is about the size of Rochester and very neat, as are all the American towns that I have seen. The principal streets are generally very wide, paved, and extend in a straight line from one end of the town to the other, but the appearance of the houses is spoilt by the inferior quality of the glass in the windows.

Friday June 20. Left Utica yesterday evening at 6.30 p.m. by boat on account of the rain, and at Schenectady left the canal and transferred to the railroad by which Albany is only 16 miles, whereas it is upwards of thirty by canal. The railroad starts up a long steep hill performed by locomotive machinery. One end of a long rope is attached at the top of the hill to a heavy carriage laden with stone, and the other end of the rope is fixed to the line of carriages which are at the bottom of the hill. There are rollers in the middle of the road for the rope to run upon, and as soon as the carriage at the top begins to descend, those at the bottom ascend at six miles an hour. At the top of the hill a steam carriage was waiting for us in which we travelled to within two miles of Albany, and then horses drew us the remainder. We performed the sixteen miles within an hour, reaching Albany at 5 p.m. It is the largest town I have seen in the States, containing about 35,000 inhabitants. There are many splendid buildings; the Capitol, the City Hall, etc. The town stands on the western side of the Hudson river, the principal part being in the valley, but it extends to the top of the hill, crowned by the Capitol. There is considerable trade, and very few poor. All the American towns have many blacks, who are employed as waiters, cooks, peregrines,* etc.
Saturday June 21. Amused myself by walking around the outskirts of the town. The wheat is looking well and is in ear. It is fine country and a farmer can make a good living; he generally drives a pair of horses abreast in a light waggon in which they convey goods to

*Vagrants without rights of citizenship.

market. The horses are what we term stiff hackneys and are for running rather than for drawing. They have no heavy cart horses.

The papers report the death of General Lafayette who was held in great esteem in this country. Orders were given by the Senate for funeral honours to be performed and a general mourning. Politics run very high here; almost everyone is a politician—they have their Whigs and Tories as in England.

Sunday June 22. More regard is paid to religion here than in the 'Old Country', as it is called; and there are more places of worship for the population than I have ever seen. This is also true of all the towns and villages that we have passed.

The ladies, of whom there are an abundance, dress very gaily, even the lower orders having their silks and satins. I suppose they are very cheap. Wine, on the other hand, is dear being about double the price it is at home. A bottle of port costs two dollars, but most people are water drinkers. Although I do not belong to the Temperance Society, I drink very little else. Liquors are cheap, not being more than a fourth of the price in England, but the Temperance Society has done wonders and there is little consumed. In my opinion there requires to be another society for the control of eating: I have never seen such gormandising; John Bull is nothing to the Yankee in this respect.

Seven per cent is given for money on good security, and a man with a wife and family may live well on the interest on about ten thousand dollars; in England the interest on twice that sum would scarcely serve him. I do not like to say anything against 'My own, my native land', but it is astonishing that Englishmen pinch and screw and deprive themselves of common necessities, when in this country they might live and enjoy themselves with independence and happiness: no Poor Rates, no Tithes, and scarcely any taxes. Society is as good as at home, and luxuries, the same, in a healthy climate, a beautiful country with noble rivers and mountains, magnificent cataracts, extensive forests, and splendid towns and rural villages; in fact a country gifted by nature with resources more numerous than any other country in the world.

Were my friends here, I should rejoice in making this country my home for the remainder of my life, and setting aside the natural feelings one has for fatherland and native soil; when settled with my wife and little ones prattling around me, I should be as happy as a prince and much more independent. Humbug—a little touch of the sun!

Monday June 23. Hot, with the thermometer 80°F in the shade. Walked to Troy, six miles up the river. It is divided into East and West Troy, separated by the river which is about four hundred yards wide. There is no connecting bridge and coaches pass from one side to the other by the Horse Ferry, which crosses continually between the two Troys. (Bye the bye I did not see traces of the renowned

Hudson City and the Catskill Mountains.

battle between the Greeks and Trojans of 3,000 years ago! The Americans are fond of borrowing ancient names for their towns: Troy, Rome, Carthage, London, Lyons, etc. . . .) Coaches run at all hours of the day between Albany and Troy, and steamboats are constantly going backwards and forwards.

In the evening I went to the theatre at Albany to see Forrest the tragedian, who is thought very much of, and he is certainly clever. The theatre excepted, I believe there is no other place for public amusement in the town.

Tuesday June 24.   The weather is still very hot. Many people visit the Saratoga Springs, about forty miles away; I suppose it is a second Cheltenham. The waters are said to be famous, and taste brackish as if there was sulphur in them. They are sold in Albany by the name of Congress Water at one shilling a bottle. My health being good I shall stay away.

Wednesday June 25.   The Hudson river at Albany is about half a mile wide and the steam vessels to New York are very large and fitted up in grand style, covering the 140 miles in a day starting at seven in the morning and arriving before night. I left for Catskill on the *Champlain,* a steamer of 200 horse power, with two fire engines having ten foot strokes. The beams work outside the vessel which gives a singular appearance. I have not seen anything similar in England. The vessel is of immense size and well fitted up, with two decks one above the other.

Top: *a Catskill village*. Above: *Mountain House*.

Twenty-eight miles from Albany we touched at Hudson, a large town on the eastern bank of the Hudson river and opposite Athens on the western side. The steamboat crews are very expeditious in landing passengers at small settlements; when there is no pier they lower a boat which hangs alongside and the passengers get in. A crewman on the vessel then pays out a rope fastened to the boat, while another crewman in the boat steers for the landing place and as soon as he has another cargo the boat is pulled back to the vessel which has been moving slowly on.

After leaving the steamer we travelled twelve miles by stage on a villainous road from Catskill town to the mountains, and on the top of one is the Mountain House, five miles up a very steep road which in parts seems almost perpendicular, and as it winds along there is a precipice on one side nearly all the way.

The mountains are covered with shrubs and trees and a profusion of myrtle, which is in full blossom and very beautiful. The mountains are rocky and trees appear to grow out of the solid rock. We were nearly five hours reaching Mountain House, and more than half the time was spent on the last five miles ascending from the foot of the mountain.

Mountain House which can accommodate 300, and is sometimes full of visitors, was almost deserted being too early in the season. The drawing room is beautifully furnished and is one of the largest I have ever seen. The dining room is likewise very large. The House stands on the brink of an immense precipice and faces east to the Hudson river. To the south is a still higher mountain; about two miles to the west are the Pine Orchard Falls, and to the north is the road to Catskill, along which we came. The eastern prospect over the river is particularly fine. Apparently you can almost throw a stone into the river which is ten miles distant, and the view includes parts of four States; and the Green Mountains to the north-east, which are very high and a tremendous distance off.

After dinner I walked down to the Falls which are two miles away. On a rock overlooking the Falls is a house of entertainment for visitors, and a path has been made down to the bottom of the Falls. The first fall is a hundred and eighty feet, and the lesser fall thirty yards lower down is eighty feet. The stream of water is small but the rock face of the first fall in the form of a half moon is tremendous. Those who are fond of gigantic scenery should come here. It is beyond all conception.

I walked under the first fall at the foot of the rock whose summit projects over thirty feet, and the sun shining on the spray creates a beautiful rainbow. When looking upwards from the foot of the lower fall the house and trees at the top are very small from the immense height.

I had hard work getting to the top again, and the weather being hot I was in an almighty sweat, but when I did get there I stood like a statue for some minutes unable to remove my eyes from the scenery below. The stream rushes on winding between banks of immense height covered with trees. Those who have not seen it cannot have the least conception of its magnificence.

The Catskill Falls. Right: *Caldwell's Landing on the Hudson.*

After entering my name in the book kept for that purpose, I left the Falls with regret and their memory will always remain with me. I met, too, with a slight accident which I shall not soon forget.

Close by the Falls is a beautiful spring of clear water, and I tried to keep my hand in it, but it was so excessively cold that my fingers were benumbed in a very short time.

Now and then in the winter a bear or two are sometimes seen on these mountains, and wildcats and wolves frequent the neighbourhood. Lately a panther has been prowling about but it is rare for any of these beasts to be seen.

Thursday June 26. Arose at five this morning and walked up the South Mountain, about five hundred feet above Mountain House, and 3,804 feet above the Hudson river. Near the top was a rock of immense size formed of small stones, but I am at a loss to explain it. When looking down on the world from the top of one of these mountains the clouds below appear like smoke or mist. It is surprising that people prefer their beds to enjoying the cool breeze of a summer's morning.

I left the mountains at 7 a.m. in a barouche drawn by a pair of fine horses, and where the road was not too rugged we went along in grand style. I breakfasted before we started, and if any meal ever had such a jolting before, I am a Yankee!

We arrived at Catskill in under two hours, and I boarded the steamer from Albany for New York, and from its deck I could see Mountain House and the South Mountain which I had ascended only a few hours before.

The Palisades on the Hudson. Right: *New York Bay from the Telegraph Station.* Below right: *the Brooklyn ferry.*

We travelled fast, sometimes going on at eighteen miles an hour, and touched at a dozen landing places. We passed several high mountains, occasional towns and villages, and here and there a gentleman's seat. The *Albany* is a fine vessel. She left the city of that name at 7 a.m. and arrived at New York at 6.30 p.m.; a distance of 140 miles including many stoppages.

Today New York performed funeral honours to the memory of Lafayette. Troops marched about the town with music and flags flying, and thousands of citizens followed in procession, while the windows of every street were filled with spectators.

Friday June 27. New York is a fine city on an island separating the Hudson river and the East river. At the southern end of the town stands the Castle, pleasantly situated; and in the park about half a mile north of the castle is the splendid City Hall. There are abundant churches and chapels for worship: eighteen Episcopal, twenty-three Presbyterian, four Catholic, eleven Baptist, ten Dutch, eleven Methodist and four Friends Places. The two principal streets are the Broadway and the Bowery. The Broadway is a noble street, two miles long and well paved. The Bowery is also a fine street, but shorter. There are two theatres, the Park and the Bowery, besides the Italian Opera and a smaller theatre. They have also their Vauxhall Gardens.

Saturday June 28. I am living at the Exchange Hotel in Broad Street, a short distance from the Broadway, capable of accommodating three

hundred persons. There are some fine hotels here; the extensive City
Hotel ranks first, and the Washington Hotel, the Atlantic and the
American are all fine buildings, and each has many respectable persons
as yearly boarders, as it is cheaper than keeping a house.
Sunday June 29. A rather gloomy wet day. The weather is much
more changeable than I had expected: for a few days it is fine and
very hot, and then two or three days of rain. Today we even have a
fire, it is so cold.

New York: the park and City Hall.

Monday June 30. There are many French residents in the city. The population of New York in 1830 was upwards of 200,000; 14,000 being blacks.

JULY

Wednesday July 2. The hottest day we have had, 86°F in the shade. Harvesting has started in some parts of the States.

Thursday July 3. I begin to be tired of having nothing to do. When I look around and see all the bustle and business, I begin to wonder why I was sent into the world, and look forward to returning to England, with the hope that I may find something to employ myself about, for an idle life is more irksome than a hard-working one. My first wish after finding my friends all well is to settle down to some business, and be a steady sober old file for the rest of my life, and if at some future period a fond simple-hearted girl should be so foolish as to fall in love with your humble servant, then I must become a Benedict; if not, be happy and contented with a bachelor's fare. If Providence should have in store a wife with lots of little brats, then when the toils of the day are over and I sit in the chimney corner with a pipe and my wife at my elbow and the little brats around us, I can tell them the sights I have seen and fight my battles over again, and send them 'weeping to their beds' (Shakespeare).

I find the Yankee gentlemen more agreeable than I had expected; they are generally well informed, and if they are not quite so polite as we are in England, other qualities they possess make up for that deficiency. They seldom speak to a stranger without first being spoken to, but when you are acquainted most are very agreeable. They have some singular ways, however, such as spitting about the floors, reaching over your plate at meals, chewing tobacco, and as soon as the dinner bell rings it is laughable to see them jump up and race to be first to the table; while as soon as each finishes, he marches off and practises upon his teeth with a toothpick, followed by a cigar, or a quid. When smoking a cigar most sit down in some place where they can put their feet on a level with their heads.

The lower orders I do not like; they are too fond of showing their independence; and rarely give a civil answer. Now I must have a touch at the ladies; all the time I have been in the States I have scarcely seen a pretty girl, much less a handsome one. They appear in poorer health than the men, and most are remarkable for the thickness of their understanding. I like them for invariably smiling at you when you meet them in the street, and not turning up their noses as do our English divinities.

Friday July 4.   This is a grand day with Us Yankees, being the 58th Anniversary of Our Independence. We make patriotic speeches, ring bells, fire cannon and smaller artillery, review troops, ascend in a balloon, and in the evening visit the Gardens where there is music and singing, laughing and plenty of courting, and grand displays of fireworks. The theatre is doubly attractive, and throughout the town are balls and pleasure parties of all descriptions.

I spent the morning at the review of the troops; the afternoon witnessing the filling of the balloon and watching it ascend majestically until the clouds hid it from sight; and the evening at the theatre. The last twenty-four hours have been a continual fusilade of squibs, crackers and pistols.

Saturday July 5.   We are quieter today. The Americans are very temperate and yesterday I scarcely saw a drunken man; on such an occasion in England we should see them rolling about the streets by the dozen.

There is no Public Corn Market here, the corn and flour being consigned to some factor. The principal streets are lighted by gas.

Sunday July 6.   Went to church.

Monday July 7.   Sheldon* arrived last evening and I met him today.

Tuesday July 8.   My hotel is very extensive with two hundred bedrooms, and about three hundred beds. Originally it was six separate houses, now thrown into one. The worthy landlord told me he pays

---

*The companion he had left at Toronto.

$7,000 per year rent, but I doubt it. English sovereigns are worth $4.80, there being 100 cents in a dollar.

Wednesday July 9. The heat has been excessive for the last five days; between 90°F and 96°F in the shade, and as high as 120°F in the sun. If one goes out in the middle of the day there is a chance of getting parboiled: and the pavements are so hot that a beef steak would broil on them. The papers report as many as thirty persons literally killed by the heat; some from imprudently drinking cold water; and several poor horses have fallen down and died in the streets. Fires are very prevalent; nearly every night that I have been here there has been one in some part of the city. The houses are chiefly five stories high, and the engines such poor things that they will only reach to the fourth story.

Thursday July 10. In this city the Whites look down upon the Blacks with the utmost contempt. The Blacks have had several meetings lately on obtaining equal rights with the Whites, and there have been several riots from some white individuals who are not prejudiced, associating with the Blacks. I see no reason why a black man is not every bit as good as a white. I doubt if their colour extends to the mind as well as the body, but I am not capable of judging.

Friday July 11. Another row last night.

Saturday July 12. Last night the mob did not confine their attacks

Philadelphia; below: *the Exchange and Giraras Bank.* Right: *the United States Bank.*

to the houses of the poor Blacks, but destroyed the inside of several of their churches. The Blacks take it very patiently. The troops are now parading about the town to put an end to these disgraceful scenes.

Sunday July 13. All quiet last night.

Monday July 14. Left New York by steamer at 10 a.m. for Philadelphia, ninety miles to the south-west. We landed at South Amboy in New Jersey, and then by railroad to Bordentown, a distance of thirty-five miles in two and a half hours: From Bordentown we took another steamer down the Delaware river and arrived at Philadelphia at six in the evening.

Tuesday July 15. Philadelphia on the Delaware river with about 200,000 inhabitants is nearly the size of New York. Visited the dockyard and saw a tremendous man-of-war being built, to carry 162 guns, at least there were that many port holes.

Wednesday July 16. Left Philadelphia by steamer at 6 a.m. for Baltimore, by way of the Delaware river as far as Newcastle, then on the railroad to Frenchtown; a distance of sixteen miles, and across the State boundary between Delaware and Maryland. The sparks from the engine were a nuisance, setting fire to sundry small clothes, gowns, etc.

At Frenchtown we again took steamer, crossing the Chesapeake Bay, and arrived at Baltimore at 3 p.m., performing the whole distance of 115 miles in nine hours. We had been in Baltimore less than 10 minutes when there was a tremendous clap of thunder and a house was struck to the ground by lightning.

Baltimore has a famous monument to Washington, 186 feet high with a statue eighteen feet on the top, the whole being composed of

Washington's Monument, Baltimore. Right: *Washington from the White House.*

marble. It has already cost $200,000, and it is expected to cost $60,000 more ere it is completed. My friend and I went to the top and had a fine view of the town and surrounding country. I believe Baltimore is the only city in the States to have any memorial worth mentioning to the renowned Washington. There is another handsome monument here commemorating a battle fought with the British in 1814, and bearing the names of the officers who were slain.

Thursday July 17. We took stage for Washington, thirty-six miles from Baltimore, and had a tremendous thunderstorm on our journey. The roads as usual were very bad. We left Baltimore at 2.30 p.m. and did not arrive at Washington until near midnight, being nine hours on the road, and I was never so tired of a journey. There were nine of us inside, and as the weather was very hot it became unpleasant.

Most of the corn along the road is already harvested, though the land appears very poor. Maryland is famous for tobacco but I have not yet seen any growing.

Friday July 18. Congress is over and Washington is almost deserted. It is a small town of scattered houses and less than 30,000 inhabitants built on the edge of the Potomac river. The Capitol stands on rising ground and is a beautiful piece of architecture, built of stone; from its top we had a fine view of the surrounding country. In the Rotunda of the Capitol are several fine paintings, including a full length portrait of Washington; a painting of the Declaration of Independence; and another of the surrender of Lord Cornwallis to the Americans. There is an extensive library open to visitors, and outside fronting the town, a beautiful marble monument with several emblematical statues.

The Capitol, Washington. Right: *a viaduct on the Baltimore and Washington railroad* Below right: *State Street, Boston.*

The House of Representatives, corresponding to our House of Commons, is well fitted up with a desk for each member and his name upon it. The seats are placed in a circle around the House. There are galleries for visitors and anyone who pleases may attend without the trouble of getting a ticket. There are about 240 members. Opposite the chair is a statue of Liberty, and a full length likeness of Lafayette was hung with crêpe.

The Senate House over which Van Buren, the Vice-president, presides, is small. I took the chair *pro tempore* just to say, 'I have sat in the chair of the Vice-president of the United States', but I did not feel any particular overflow of wisdom from so doing.

Saturday July 19. We returned to Baltimore by stage. Railroads are being built in every direction; one between Washington and Baltimore is half finished.

Saturday July 20. We left Baltimore for Philadelphia at 6 a.m. by steamer on a different line from that by which we came, and instead of travelling by railroad to Newcastle we were conveyed by stage to the city of Delaware. We arrived about 3.30 p.m. at Philadelphia.

Monday July 21. We left by steamer* at 10.30 a.m. for New York arriving at 6.30 p.m. In places there was only one track on the railroad and about half way we met a line of carriages and were obliged to wait until they came up at a part where there were two tracks; they

*Apparently changing at Bordentown to the railroad.

accidentally derailed and were delayed for some time, detaining us as well.

Wednesday July 23. *En voyage* to Boston in Massachusetts, 220 miles from New York via the East River, through Hell Gate and Long Island Sound, along the Connecticut coast to Newport, Rhode Island where we landed some passengers and took on others, and then travelled through the night arriving at nine next morning at Providence.

Thursday July 24. Took stage for Boston at 10 a.m. arriving at 5 p.m. The land alongside the road is stony and not very fertile, and the field fences are made of loose stone, while most of the houses are built of granite.

Boston is a large town of 100,000 inhabitants. The streets are less regular than in the other towns I have visited in the States. There is a fine harbour and at Charleston, which adjoins Boston, is a navy yard with a famous dry dock built of granite. Near Boston is Bunker Hill, the site of a battle in the revolution. I visited the monument there, which is less than half finished.

There appears to be considerable rivalry between the different States; the inhabitants of each thinking theirs to be better than the surrounding ones. An old lady on Bunker Hill amused me: a Yankee with me was enquiring of her about the buildings in Boston. When she learned that we were strangers from New York she told us that she guessed it would take us a twelvemonth to see over the town, appearing to think there was not another such place in the world.

Friday July 25. There is a stone bridge across the Charles river at Boston a mile and a quarter long, and lower down the river another shorter one which carries the railroad to Worcester.

Saturday July 26. Left Boston by stage at noon and arrived at Providence at 8.30 p.m. as the day was very hot, 96°F in the shade and we were obliged to give the poor horse plenty of time. Apparently

Below: *Boston and Bunker Hill.* Right: *Faneuil Hall, Boston.*

this summer is peculiarly hot, and last week the heat has been excessive.

Sunday July 27. Providence, the capital of Rhode Island, is a very pretty place with two handsome colleges built of brick on the top of a hill outside the town. I believe all the states east of the Hudson river are known as New England, and the inhabitants of the United States are divided into Southerners, the Down Easters, and the Westerners.

Monday July 28. I left Providence at noon on the *Benjamin Franklin,* steamboat for New York.

Tuesday July 29. Arrived at 6 a.m. this morning in New York, and have arranged to sail for England on Friday.

AUGUST

Friday August 1. We sailed from New York for Liverpool in the ship *Orpheus,* captain Bursley. We are in the Gulf Stream, a current which runs about three and a half knots from the Gulf of Mexico to the Mediterranean, and the water is remarkably warm. I saw several small fish called Portuguese Man-of-war*; they are light pink and travel by a fin sail which they can raise or lower at will; also a small shark three or four feet long.

---

*The creature described here is probably not a Portuguese Man-of-war, but another jellyfish *Velella*, which, according to *McClane's Standard Fishing Encyclopedia*, is 'a by-the-wind sailor, which has a flat, oval gelatinous plate . . . while the upper surface bears a transparent, triangular sail'.

A West Indiaman; from an etching by E. W. Cooke in the National Maritime Museum, Greenwich. The Orpheus *was a similar vessel.*

Tuesday August 6. Latitude 39° 49'. Longitude 59° 31'. We have had three days of very dirty weather, and the ship is crammed with passengers; there are forty-two cabin class and about two hundred and forty in the steerage. The latter is very small and there is no room to move. I have never spent five days like the last, but now the weather is fine again and a nice breeze from the west is taking us along at about ten knots. We are about one third of the distance across, and within a fortnight should be in Liverpool.

Saturday August 10. Longitude 50° 45'. We were becalmed for 36 hours, but now have a fair wind. *6 p.m.* The weather has changed, wind about north-west and it is as cold as the coldest winter day in England, probably from being near the Banks.

Sunday August 11. Longitude 46° 31'. The weather was blustery last night and still very cold.

Thursday August 15. We were becalmed nearly all Monday night, but on Tuesday the wind changed to blow from the south-west and has continued ever since taking us along at 10, 11, 12, and sometimes

13 knots. We are now about 1,030 miles from Liverpool.

Friday August 16.   The wind changed this morning to the north-east, which is unfavourable as our course is nearly due east, nevertheless we are making nearly 7 knots on our course.

Saturday August 17.   Longitude 33°. Latitude 48°. The wind is still north-east. We bespoke the ship *Eliza* from Quebec for London, out 22 days.

Sunday August 18.   The wind is still ahead.

Monday August 19.   The wind has changed from north-east to north.

Tuesday August 20.   A squall came from the north at 3 a.m. Being short of hands we were too slow in getting sail in. *11 a.m.* Spoke the ship *Hull* from Savanna for Liverpool. She is a Yankee, and being to windward of us nearly ran us down through the lubberly conduct of both captains.

Wednesday August 21.   The wind is now nearly south-west, and blowing a gale. We lost our starboard fore-top studdingsail yard before we could get the sail in; and have been under double reefed topsails for some time. The sea is running as high as I have ever seen it. *5 p.m.* We are now in the Irish Channel and the Dungarvan Mountains are in sight about fifty miles away.

Thursday August 22.   The Irish coast is still in sight. *12 noon.* The Welsh coast appeared on the starboard side. We expected to make port tonight, but will be disappointed.

Friday August 23.   Last night a bit of a gale sprang up off Anglesea, and for the first time in the whole course of the voyage I felt alarmed, knowing that the Irish Channel is dangerous, and having a poor opinion of our captain's skill as a seaman I considered our situation unenviable. We made out for mid channel, and laid to until morning when at 5.30 a.m. the pilot came aboard and took us to Liverpool by 12 noon.

The Mersey at Liverpool.

The Lighthouse at Sunderland.

China
and Back
1857

Alexander Whitehead

The Vanguard *of 626 tons, was built in 1857 at Sunderland by William Pile for J. Kelso and registered at Shields. She was built of wood, sheathed with yellow metal and copper fastened; A1 at Lloyds. It is curious that young Whitehead does not tell us that his ship was on her maiden voyage, or mention her master, Captain Scott, by name.*

Alexander Whitehead was seventeen when he signed articles on June 2, 1857, to sail from Sunderland to Shanghai in the Vanguard. *Nineteen years later he became chief engineer of the* Halle, *lost with all hands in 1876 in the Bay of Biscay. He left a wife and small son.*

The account of his first voyage is written in Northumbrian dialect and his own spelling; and though attractive in manuscript, is disconcerting in print; with a few colourful exceptions the text has been transcribed into standard English.

Plates from Captain H. Paasch's Illustrated Marine Encyclopedia *(1890) have been reproduced in* Appendix A *to assist readers with the descriptions of the sails, sheets and spars.*

The engravings of the English coast used to illustrate this and the other diaries are taken from Finden's Ports, Harbours and Watering Places, *and the Chinese scenes from Wright's* China *(1843).*

Young Whitehead describes the everyday life of the crew of a small ship at sea. His simple story has no epic moment; but through his pen the Vanguard *represents innumerable forgotten ships which served their generation well.*

The Vanguard *by a Chinese artist; a painting brought home by Alexander Whitehead for his mother. A damaged label on the back of the frame reads:*

C	QUA	*possibly:*	C	QUA
S	TRAIT		SHIP	PORTRAIT
	\INTER		ARTIST & PAINTER

Right: *serving a rope.*

The *Vanguard's* passage Shanghai to London in 103 days compares well with those of crack tea-clippers of nearly twice her tonnage. The *Thermopylae* of 991 tons sailed from Shanghai to London four times; in 1873 taking 101 days; in 1874, 101 days; in 1877, 104 days; and in 1878 110 days.

In comparing records, the time of sailing is important; ships sailing at the end of June or beginning of July had the full strength of the SW monsoon against them, whereas later in the year the favourable NE monsoon carried them down the China Seas. The times of the tea-clippers taking part in the great Tea Race of 1868 sailing from Shanghai may also be of interest.

Forward Ho sailed June 11, arrived October 17 — days out 128
Titania sailed June 13, arrived October 17 — days out 126
Leander sailed June 13, arrived September 30 — days out 109
Taitsing sailed June 15, arrived October 19 — days out 126

JUNE 1857

Sunday June 14. We left the land early this morning with a fair wind from the SE. We have a sea-pie* for dinner today, and I intend to eat my whack if it is good, which I hope it will be.

Set studdingsails and went to our tea. I broached my spice loaf, and we had a comfortable tea. I have finished my spicenuts. We have been going 10 to 12 knots today.

Monday June 15. We close reefed our topsails early this morning and stowed the jib, and shortly after stowed all the mizen sails and hauled up the mainsail and foresail.

Tuesday June 16. Set sail this morning with a fine wind right aft; our foresail and mizen topsail close reefed. Tom† lay in bed all last night, but he had some rice today which made him better. We spoke to a ship this afternoon.

Wednesday June 17. Light winds and fine weather. All hands about the rigging.

Thursday June 18. Fine weather with a stiff breeze. Had duff and treacle today for dinner. Our watch has been serving ropes and such like.**

*Sea-pie is described in a cookery book of 1870 as a pie made from scraps. Pieces of salt beef and vegetables were boiled together in a pan, and covered with suet or dripping pastry, then the whole pie was simmered for an hour or more.

†The other apprentice.

**Binding a rope with spunyarn as a protection against wear and weather.

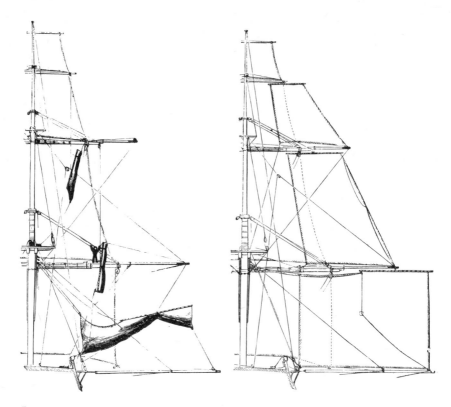

Lower, topmast, and topgallant studdingsails.

Friday June 19. At 3 a.m. set the royals and starboard fore topmast and lower studdingsails. At 6 a.m. the wind scanted.* Took in the lower studdingsails. It fell calm in the evening and we had nothing to do all night. I finished my loaf.

Saturday June 20. Very hot and calm; the crew have been scraping and greasing the masts today, and I have been varnishing the spare topmast and studdingsail booms.

Sunday June 21. Light wind and fine weather from the sw. Tom and I were called on the poop to take the sun and found ourselves in Latitude 34° 24′ 35″ N.† We had a sea-pie for dinner, but so salt we could not eat it.

Monday June 22. Tacked ship at 8 a.m. Little wind and very warm. The others tarring tarpaulins which is a nasty job. Played Tom a few games at draughts and I won them all.

Tuesday June 23. I have been painting dead eyes and blocks which is a nice job for a hot day. Sighted Madeira.

*Old Norse *skant*—short, scanty; hence Northumbrian scanted.
†A little south of Gibraltar.

Wednesday June 24. Set our starboard fore studdingsails. Saw a shark and put a hook over but he didn't want a tow.
Thursday June 25. Still calm; part of the crew have been working with ropes, and the others painting. I was a painter. The carpenter cut both his feet. We passed close to Madeira.
Friday June 26. A scanty wind which helped us on a little.
Saturday June 27. Into the Trades and set all the studdingsails. A flying fish came on board to save its life.
Sunday June 28. Saw the Canary Islands at 5 a.m. Tom and I were invited out to dinner. We had soup and bully [?],* sea-pie, roast beef, and potatoes, plum pudding and sauce; a very good dinner for such a day.

We exchanged signals with the *Ellen Gibben* from London bound for the Straits of Sunday.† She has been 26 days out, and we only 19.
Tuesday June 30. Setting up the rigging. Our maintopgallant-studdingsail halliards broke this morning.

JULY

Wednesday July 1. We finished the rigging and were set odd jobs. Came out of the Trades.
Thursday July 2. Tom and I were set to pick thrums** out of the shaking bag for the matmakers.
Friday July 3. Light winds and cloudy. The carpenter finished the poop in fine style.
Saturday July 4. Scraped the resin off the poop, and started with the mats. At 5 p.m. washed the decks and cleaned the houses out for Sunday.
Sunday July 5. Nothing to do all day but read and fish. Towards night it rained so we caught some water.
Monday July 6. I had a large wash today; the first since we left Sunderland.
Tuesday July 7. Light and variable winds with drops of rain. This afternoon I was down in the forecastle when I heard a noise on deck. I came up and ran to the poop where they had a shark hooked. We hauled him in and ran him down on the main deck where we soon cut him up and had part cooked for tea; it was very good.
Wednesday July 8. Exchanged signals with the *Anny Chesyse.*
Sunday July 12. Light winds for the last few days, but fresh today from the s and w with passing squalls and rain. We had a long talk with the *Viceroy.*

*Here, as in other places, the diary is stained and illegible.
†The Straits of Sunda, between Sumatra and Java.
**Loose threads.

Monday July 13. Strong breeze and cloudy with rain. Tom spilt his peasoup this afternoon.

Thursday July 16. One of the men and I were up serving the main topgallant footropes.

Friday July 17. On the royal yard at the same work.

Saturday July 18. Served the foreroyal footropes.

Sunday July 19. Tom and I passed the day very comfortably drawing ships.

Monday July 20. We crossed the Line* last night about 10 o'clock, but knew nothing about it until this morning.

Tuesday July 21. Set our studdingsails early this morning, and shortly afterwards took them in. The steward's leg was so bad this morning that I had to be his mate.

Thursday July 23. Had to rub the fingermarks off the cabin which I did not like.

Friday July 24. The steward had to scrub the cabin out, at which he growled very hard and talked about his game leg.

Saturday July 25. Scrubbed the paintwork all round the ship. I left the cabin just before dinner and I was very glad for a revolution broke out. The cook was unshipped† for being dirty, and the steward got palpitation of the heart.

Sunday July 26. The cook has been down-hearted all day and I don't think he spoke to anyone. Tom and I had a glass of wine with sugar and warm water which was very nice.

Monday July 27. We took the opportunity to bend the sails for there was very little wind.

Thursday July 30. Today I was converted into a glazier, and set to putty the waterways round the poop and fill all the little holes.

Friday July 31. At the same work. We passed to the west of Trinidad about 2 p.m. There is a strong breeze from the west.

AUGUST

Saturday August 1. Finished the putty work on the poop and started with the maindeck. It fell calm towards night.

Sunday August 2. We have been accompanied by a shoal of whales all day.

Monday August 3. Calm all day. We had a fine game at hunt the slipper in the dog watch, which ended with black eyes and bloody noses.**

*The equator.
†Dismissed from his post.
**A children's game where a slipper is hidden and the players have to find it. Presumably here a member of the crew hid another's clothing and a fight resulted.

Tuesday August 4.   Strong breezes from the ESE. We had a game of Countrymen Coming to Trade*. I bent a guernsey† for it is getting cold.

Wednesday August 5.   Two cape pigeons have been flying after us.

Friday August 7.   The galley smoked very hard which made the cook swear.

Saturday August 8.   Strong breezes and cloudy; it came on to blow at night and carried away the weather main royal sheet, and broke the main topgallant staysail tack.

Sunday August 9.   The day has been fine but came on a raining about 7. Took the royals in, and set them about 8 o'clock. I used the last of my butter.

Tuesday August 11.   The ex-cook appeared on deck for the first time since he lost his billet.

Thursday August 13.   My watch below this morning, and I made some spicenuts which were very nice, all they wanted was ginger. The cook and the mate were farding** for pigeons and caught one.

Friday August 14.   We set the pigeon adrift with the ship's name round his neck.

Saturday August 15.   We exchanged signals with a Dutchman, and soon came alongside and had a long talk together. I saw a large albatross.

Sunday August 16.   It started to blow and rain very hard just before dinner, making us take in the main topgallant studdingsail. We are south of the Cape,†† scudding along for warm weather. The men put me in the dog basket, and set me down and I could not move one way or the other. As night came on it began to blow, and we took in our royals and topgallant studdingsails. It still increased and we took in the lower and topmast studdingsails, the topgallantsails, and rolled up a little of the topsails, and stowed the mainsail and spanker.

Monday August 17.   Set all sail this morning, and the studdingsails on the starboard side. The weather is squally with rain. A sea came into the house last night, and nearly washed Tom and me out of our bunks, and we had to keep bailing all night.

Tuesday August 18.   A stiff breeze blowing all day.

Wednesday August 19.   We exchanged signals with an American, and later fell in with ice and had to set a lookout. I have been making a ditty box‡ this afternoon. Set port fore topmast and lower studding-sails.

*There seems to be no other reference to this game.
†Put on a sweater. Bend is used throughout the diary in the nautical sense of fixing or putting on.
**Painting bird-lime on a mast or spar.
††The Cape of Good Hope.
‡Seaman's box for odds and ends, sewing material, letters, etc.

Thursday August 20.   We are rolling along with studdingsails on both sides. I have not had much to do today. The ex-cook has been teazing oakum – there is always some kind of a job.

Friday August 21.   One of our beautiful able seamen had a row with the mate this morning.

Friday August 22.   The wind has been very variable. I have been down in the forecastle helping the Old Man.*

Sunday August 23.   We have had some heavy hail squalls, and I can hardly keep my seat; she is rolling heavily and our house is full of water. Last night was the coldest yet. We took in all sail but the topsails close-reefed, and foresails.

Monday August 24.   Last night when Tom and I were bailing out the house, I opened the door to empty a bucket and a great sea came over the rail and into the house, which made me lose my wind for it was rather cooling; and it wet most of the things in my chest, and washed Tom's blanket; he had to turn into my bunk.

Tuesday August 25.   We spoke a ship from Shields bound for Hong Kong. She had carried away her main topsail yard. The dogs got hold of Ander's oilskin jacket and tore the back out for pastime.

Wednesday August 26.   We tacked ship four times today. I have been darning stockings this afternoon.

Thursday August 27.   The carpenter has been making wedges† for our big guns, and put lead covers over the touch holes.

Friday August 28. We have been making French sennit** for bunt gaskets for the royals.

Saturday August 29.   Still squally and unsettled. I have been dodging the boatswain for I could not bother to do much work.

Sunday August 30.   It has been fine and I put my bed out to air as it was damp. We set our studdingsails on the starboard side to help us along.

Monday August 31.   Our main topgallant stay gave way.

SEPTEMBER

Tuesday September 1.   We took 50 baskets of coals from aft and put them down forr'd. The old lady†† has had one of her fits, and was sent to the lunatic asylum.

---

*The captain.
†Probably chocks to prevent movement.
**Plaited cord. There are different forms of sennit according to the method of plaiting. Bunt gaskets were used to fasten a furled sail to the yard, and were often in the form of a net.
††One of the dogs on board.

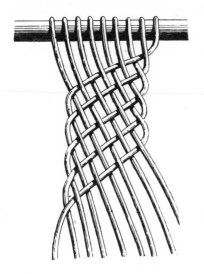 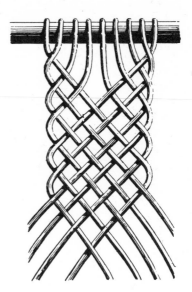

Left: *English sennit*. Right: *French sennit*.

Wednesday September 2. Sent the fore topgallant studdingsail booms and mizen royal up, and set all the studdingsails.

Thursday September 3. We passed Amsterdam,* but were too far north to see it. Started the manropes† today.

Friday September 4. Continued the same work. Hazy and calm all day.

Saturday September 5. The boatswain started the yoke ropes** for the gig.

Sunday September 6. We had fun with the albatrosses and pigeons by tying fat meat on bits of string and tossing them overboard. One would pick up a piece and fly away, and another would catch hold of the other end and pull him back. There would be a fight, and an albatross would come and settle the dispute by scoffing the lot.

Monday September 7. Plenty of small rain and light winds. We exchanged signals with a four-masted Dutchman who very soon left us. I had a small wash today.

Wednesday September 9. A strong breeze this morning increased by degrees and we close reefed the topsail. Hickerty and Helman were skylarking at teatime and Hickerty's knife stuck in Helman's leg. Helman is laid up.

*Amsterdam Island in the Indian Ocean.
†Life-lines rigged for bad weather.
**Ropes for working the rudder.

Thursday September 10. One of the men caught a little bird† swimming along the deck and gave it to me. I made a roly-poly pudding for dinner; it was not boiled enough, but very good for all that. The weather is squally.

Friday September 11. We were plashing among the rain all last night, which was very pleasant. We are going along with our single reefed topsails and coursers. My petrel is very lively, and I had him on deck getting his wings in order.

Saturday September 12. I let the bird go. The old dog took one of her fits again so she was set aswimming.

Sunday September 13. A fine day and I put my bedding out to air.

Monday September 14. We started to rattle the rigging down. I have been making putty wholesale.

Tuesday September 15. The men are at the same work, and Tom and I were sent to putty the seams round the outside of the poop.

Wednesday September 16. We finished the putty work on the poop and the mate painted it.

Thursday September 17. The mate and I painted manropes.

Friday September 18. The fore topmast studdingsail halliards gave way this morning. We put both anchors over the bows today. It started to blow and we took in all the studdingsails and royals.

Saturday September 19. The water turned very white about 12 last night so we clewed up the topgallantsails and lowered the topsails down and tried to get soundings, but there was no bottom and we set the sails again. We bent the cables on the anchors this afternoon; and passed a man-of-war about 6 p.m.

Sunday September 20. We have been looking out for land all day and at 5 p.m. saw it right ahead, so we put her under easy canvas to dodge about till daylight.

Monday September 21. We sighted Java ahead, and there is a vast number of small islands besides. It is very pleasant sailing amongst them for the water is smooth. One of the men caught a fine booby† on the flyingboom end. I was catching loggerheads** which was good fun.

Tuesday September 22. Our hottest day. Potter killed his booby and and gave me the wings, but I don't think they are worth keeping. We started to paint the boats.

Wednesday September 23. A French frigate steamed close by us, but said nothing. There were about half a dozen middies standing on the bridge, but she was very dirty.

The master of the barque *Strathmoor* came on board and had tea.

*A petrel: see below.
†A sea bird related to the gannet.
**Carnivorous turtles.

He brought a dozen chickens, some bananas and sweet potatoes, and two cocoanuts. The mate gave me a banana which I liked very much.
Thursday September 24. We left our friend last night. I had some green cocoanut and two bananas, which were very nice; and we had sweet potatoes for dinner. I liked them very well.

We have been preparing our guns ready for pirates;* but when we tried the balls they were over large, so we made slugs out of bolts and bits of copper lashed together.
Friday September 25. Painting and sailorising to make her smart before we reach Hong Kong. We waited this afternoon for our friend to come up to us and gave him a salute with both the guns.
Saturday September 26. We crossed the Line about noon, and passed Direction Island at 4 p.m. They are two fine little islands and full of trees. The steward killed two chickens.
Sunday September 27. Tom and I had dinner in the cabin; first course was soup and bouilli, second boiled mutton and yam, then we had our mouths tickled with roast chicken, for I think I could polish four with ease, and finished with plum pudding. There was a tart but it was not cut. The master was invited to dine on the *Strathmore,* but her gig and ours were both fresh painted and he did not go.
Monday September 28. Captain Mann was on board again today; he took two casks of water for they were rather short, and brought a basket of eggs for the master.
Tuesday September 29. We are having a hard match with our 15 knot companion, but I think we can beat him for we have kept company since he came up with us.
Wednesday September 30. Our little dog died last night. It turned squally with rain, and all hands were called.

OCTOBER

Friday October 1. The weather unchanged and we sent the fore and mizenroyal yards down. Our friend is out of sight.
Friday October 2. A fine calm day. A shark has been swimming around us and we tried to catch him but could not.
Saturday October 3. We caught him about 4 a.m. and cut him up and I had some for my breakfast and tea. This is Tom's 16th birthday.
Sunday October 4. There is a breeze but the wrong way. The master says if it were stronger we could beat up to our port in ten days.
Monday October 5. We sent the royal yards up this morning. Our friend the *Strathmoor* is not far from us. I caught a beautiful ring dove about 7 p.m.

*See Appendix E

Junks and a fishing boat off the coast of China. Right: *the harbour at Hong Kong.*

Tuesday October 6. The mate and I made a cage for him this morning, and he is very lively and tame. A breeze has come which is very welcome. There was a dove on the fore topsail, but everybody wanted him and nobody got him.

Wednesday October 7. It is very hot and the wind light. My turtle dove remains lively. Potter caught another fine booby tonight.

Thursday October 8. I caught a kind of swallow this morning and let it go again; then the master caught it and gave it to me, and I put him in my bunk, but he died and I skinned him.

Friday October 9. We caught another shark about five feet long, and cut him open but there was nothing in his bags. He was tossed overboard except the jaws and backbone. There are plenty of dolphins about, but we cannot catch any. The cook speared a big one with the graines* but he shook himself off before anyone could get hold of him.

Saturday October 10. My dove has been very sulky and I took him out of the cage. He was quite tame, and was brisk again in the afternoon. Potter caught another live booby.

Sunday October 11. The dove has been in the same humour all day so I gave him liberty to walk about. There is a fine breeze tonight.

Monday October 12. When I looked at my bird this morning he was dead so I skinned him intending to stuff the skin, but I spoiled it. I took the sun today and found we were in Latitude 17° 14′ 23″ N.

*A term sometimes applied to cattle with bloated stomachs.

There is a fine breeze and we expect to arrive in a few days.

Tuesday October 13. The wind is ENE and heavy clouds. At 2 p.m. tacked ship, and furled the royals about 7 p.m.

Wednesday October 14. Potter caught a dove and gave it to me but it is not as pretty as the last.

Thursday October 15. There are twelve junks in sight but a good way off. About 2 p.m. the dove escaped from the cage and settled on the jibstay and stopped there nearly all afternoon, and then shifted to a better place before dark. We went up to catch him but he was too wide awake and flew away.

Friday October 16. We sighted the Asses Ears about 4 a.m. and entered port* at 2 p.m. We were besieged with Chinese and had to cut many of their boats away. The men-of-war were firing nearly all day.†

Saturday October 17. We hauled the boats up to the davits and spread the awnings. Four ships have left today. I bought some bananas and eggs.

Sunday October 18. I bought some curios and fruit. Nobody has gone on shore which is a pity. Tom and I wanted to go. Three ships have left and two came in.

Monday October 19. We sent the topgallant yards down and put the

---

*Hong Kong; already a major port. In 1853 there were 240 ship's chandlers, 12 rope manufacturers and 2 cannon foundries. By 1858 the numbers had increased. In 1857 some 1,700 ocean-going ships entered and cleared the harbour, totalling nearly a million tons.

†In 1857 and 1858 there were naval operations against the growing menace of pirates. The second Anglo-Chinese war was also in progress. See Appendix E.

gear away. We had a very nice piece of roast beef for dinner today; much less tough than yesterday's.

Tuesday October 20.   We struck the fore and mizen topgallant masts and unbent all the sails but the jibs, staysails and spanker. Coolies are working the coals. They started today and say they will get them out in a fortnight, but I doubt it for they have only moved 33 tons today. The cook has his old berth again and is as proud as a dog with two tails.

Wednesday October 21.   There are eight carpenters caulking. Tom and I had to keep a look-out at dinner-time to stop the coolies stealing anything, but one of them walked off with a brass belaying pin and I did not see him; when the mate found out you can imagine what we got.

Thursday October 22.   Struck the main topgallant mast and sent the gear down. There is a tea-party in the cabin.

Friday October 23.   A very fine day but the coal dust has been flying all over. We sent the main topgallant mast up. After tea I had a fine bathe.

Saturday October 24.   We had a job to wash the decks after the coolies had gone. Tom and I got liberty to go on shore; he had two dollars and I had one. We had a fine bathe over the side.

Below: *a Chinese boatman with melons, and fishermen using cormorants; a ring round the bird's neck prevents it from swallowing the fish.* Above right: *playing at shuttlecock with the feet.* Below right: *a bamboo aqueduct at Hong Kong.*

Sunday October 25. Tom and I went on shore with the carpenter, but fell in with some of the crew and left him; had our dinner and then left the crew and strolled about the mountains. When we came into the town we fell in with the second and third mates and steward, and then we met the carpenter drunk. We walked towards the boat but the carpenter broke down one of the small trees that grow in the streets, and a policeman gave him lodgings for the night. All the men came on board sober except one.

An itinerant barber. Right: *a cap-vendor's shop.*

I bought a pair of Chinese slippers and Tom a fan. The *Antagonist* came in today; the barque we spoke that had sprung her mainyard.
Monday October 26.   The carpenter had to pay £2 for the tree. He was let out in the afternoon. I felt tired after my walk and did not do much work. The carpenters started to caulk the decks. The mail came in today and I have been writing my letter.
Tuesday October 27.   We stowed 150 bags of goods today; no coals have been taken out. The cook set the galley on fire, and if it had not been seen in time the ship would have been a wreck in a few minutes. The second mate and I started to paint the carved work about our head.* A boat ran against our stern and carried away her foremast.
Wednesday October 28.   I sent my letter on shore and expect the mail will leave tonight. I tasted pumpkin pie; it is very nice.
Thursday October 29.   The cook set the back of the galley on fire again. Jim and Bob went on shore yesterday and came back drunk. We finished the gilt work on the starboard side of the head and quarter. Tom has not been very well today and stopped in his bunk.
Friday October 30.   We took on 583 bags of sugar, and I had to keep tally. The master of the *Antagonist* is on board to tea.

*The figure head and scroll work at the bows of the *Vanguard* were by John Lindsay, the leading carver of the day, who was commanded by Queen Victoria to decorate Windsor Castle. Lindsay was very proud of his title, 'Carver and Gilder by appointment to H.M. Queen Victoria'.

Saturday October 31. We loaded 270 boxes of dried fruit, and a lot of wood which had a funny stink. The waterboat has been alongside and filled our fore tank.

NOVEMBER

Sunday November 1. A very fine day but nobody has been on shore. Tom and I went and looked in one of the boxes to see what was in it, and took three out. They were in shells and tasted like raisins.*

Monday November 2. Nearly everyone has diarrhoea, and the second mate had to go to bed. The coolies stowed away a lot of bags of something.† I have been keeping tally of the coals nearly all day. This morning the misses and kids of the coal lighter were roasting rats for their breakfast.

Tuesday November 3. I was keeping tally of the rice and a thousand bags were put in, and I don't know how many pieces of wood.

The steward was sent on board the *Antagonist* to see how the steward there waited at table, and I had to set the tea in our cabin; I had a taste of everything there was, and plenty of butter and sugar with my biscuit.

Wednesday November 4. All our coal is out which is good, and 100

---

*Possibly lychees.

†This may have been opium: there was a trade in the drug between Hong Kong and Shanghai.

Cat merchants and tea dealers. Right: *a lantern merchant's show room.*
Below right: *Hong Kong from Kowloon.*

bags of rice and 244 boxes of dried fruit in. The carpenter has taken to his bed again very bad. They bent the foresail.

Thursday November 5. We have taken in 1176 bags of 'lice' as the coolies call it; 120 bags of herbs, 50 bags of cloves, and 43 heavy boxes. We bent the mizen topsail.

Friday November 6. Today had 979 bags of rice, 325 of herbs, 274 of sugar, 52 of cloves, and 55 of rubbish country pitch. The second mate has been on deck doing a few little jobs. Five fingered Jack brought my jacket and trousers, and I paid a dollar. The waterboat has filled the two tanks aft.

Saturday November 7. I got out of bed with a very sore throat, but it got better towards night and my nose is running hard. We took on 750 bags of rice, 25 of mats, and eight great stones one ton weight. I have been in some of the lighters looking at josses.*

Sunday November 8. Tom, the boatswain and I were on shore and I bought a little carved wood box† for George, but I think it cost too much; I gave two dollars for it. I had my little jacket and white trousers on.

*Chinese religious figures.
†His descendants still have this box, together with the curios and slippers mentioned earlier.

Monday November 9. We sent the topgallant yards and sails up and bent the main topmast staysail. The steward has been away this afternoon and I had to set the tea. We took on 400 bags of sugar, and 350 boxes of something very light.

Tuesday November 10. We took on 600 bags of rice and 36 boxes, some containing wine. Helman went on shore with the cook on liberty. The cook came on board about 6 p.m. drunk, with the carpenter. He had not been on board long when he took a fit which lasted two hours, and took six men to hold him all the time. The mate was giving him some physic in a teacup, but as soon as it touched his lips he seized it and bit a great lump out.

I have been along with the steward to help as he had a large party to tea. I bought two canaries.

Wednesday November 11. We have shipped 420 bags of rice, which has filled us up. We bent the fore and main topsails, mainsail and cross-jack.

Thursday November 12. We hoisted the salt beef flag*, put the boats on the beam and a vast more little jobs, such as lashing casks and anything that will roll about. I wrote a letter last night.

Friday November 13. We only took on 60 boxes of something; and a lot of fowls and two little piebald pigs and some fruit. The *Fairy Queen* left for Shanghai. Tom fell overboard but caught hold of a cable.

Saturday November 14. I paid the washerwife a dollar for my washing, and she fetched me a jar of ginger which will never see home! I have been helping the steward to clean the cabin.

Sunday November 15. The mate was aboard the *Antagonist* and he fetched a nice little monkey. Tom and I have had a bathe; the last we will have until we get into warm weather. I have bent my blankets.

Monday November 16. We got under way about 6 a.m. with little wind and fine weather. The pilot left us at 1 p.m. Took in the top-gallantsail at 8 p.m. and reefed the topsails.

Tuesday November 17. The weather is still fine with a heavy sea on, and nearly everyone has felt rather funny.

Wednesday November 18. We unrolled a little of the mizen topsail, and set the main topgallantsails, and took in the slack of the lee mainrigging. At 8 p.m. set the main topgallant staysail, fore top-gallantsail and flying jib, and shortly after took all in but the topsails and courses.

Thursday November 19. We tacked ship at noon; she lay up NW by N.

Friday November 20. The weather is still the same – as soon as we make sail it starts to blow and we have to take it in again. Tacked ship at 2 p.m. and she lay N by W.

Saturday November 21. The weather has moderated and we unrolled a little of the main and mizen topsails. Set the three topgallantsails, flying jib and main topgallant staysail. The mate and I had a fine laugh. We were sitting in the house and the boatswain put his hand

*The meaning of this phrase is not clear; there may be an error in the transcription.

into his pocket and said, pulling out a handfull of cherry skins, 'What the deuce is that?' and when he tried the other it was full too!

Sunday November 22. I have been reading a book called *A Whim and its Consequences* all day. We had the best pudding since we left home. We took in all the little sails last night, but the main top-gallantsail, and set them all again today, and unrolled the reefs out of the topsails. The lamp is having fine fun blinking just to hinder me from writing. It is a beautiful night, and my eight hours below, which is beautiful too!

Monday November 23. We shifted bags of rice forr'd, and took some light boxes of fruit aft to make her sail better.

Tuesday November 24. We passed a barque something like the *Fairy Queen*. Took in all the little sails and rolled one reef in the topsails. There is a strong swell on and she is daubing her bows in.

Thursday November 26. A lookout has been kept all day. We sighted the Bashee Islands* at daybreak and passed them about noon. It blew hard towards night and we took in all the small sails and rolled a little of the topsails up.

Friday November 27. The wind dropped a little and we set the main topgallantsail and shortly after the fore one. Tom and I had some very good games of checkers.

Saturday November 28. A vast of bonito beside our bows; we tried to catch some, but the first one that hooked fell off just as he was hauled up to the jib-boom.

Sunday November 29. It fell calm last night and we had plenty of yard drill for what wind there was flew about. The steward gave Tom and me some oranges and bananas.

Monday November 30. There has been a breeze aft all day, but a strong head sea is stopping us.

DECEMBER

Tuesday December 1. A calm, sleety day. I found a piece of soap' in the dough; we expect to be poisoned some day. We set up the main rigging. Jackoe† has stolen the sugar twice out of my cage.

Wednesday December 2. Tom had a row with one of the men last night called John Jobson. He called Tom's brother something, and Tom said he would stick up for him, and he knocked Jobson down with a pump handle. A squall took us at 7 a.m. and we called all hands to shorten sail. It was quite calm before.

Thursday, December 3. All sail set but the wind is foul.

*South-east of Formosa.
†The monkey.

Eastern and Western shipping off the Ning-po estuary. Right: *Yin-shan or Silver Island on the Yangtse.*

Friday, December 4. A large flock of sparrows and some other kind of birds visited us. I caught two sparrows.

Saturday December 5. The men have been very religious today on their knees scrubbing the decks with the prayer books.* We passed three ships to windward. I caught the monkey stealing sugar out of the birdcage and I gave him a lambasting. It was very cold last night.

Sunday December 6. The wind has been in the right quarter, but very little of it. We had salt horse dough and yams for our dinner, but the latter were all bad.

Monday December 7. I had a fit† of the same kind that I had about a year ago at Tynemouth; and I bit my tongue end nearly off, so I was given chicken broth for dinner. The weather has been the same with a 4-knot breeze.

Tuesday, December 8. A nice breeze this morning and we sighted land. There were thousands of boats. We took in all sail but the three topsails, and dodged about till daylight and then set them all again.

Wednesday December 9. A Yankee pilot came on board at 11 a.m. and we sailed a good way up. Just before we were going to let go the anchor he ran us aground which kept us working until dark, for we had to hoist the pinnace out and run a cadge** away astern. I bent my new shoes for I was hard up.

*Holystones.
†This description suggests that he was a mild epileptic.
**Kedge: a secondary anchor carried out to deep water in a boat. The cable was taken to the windlass and the ship hauled off.

Thursday December 10.   Raining all day. We weighed anchor at 6 a.m., and brought up at 11 a.m.; lifted again about 4 p.m. and let go at, dark. Clewed up the topsails and stowed the topgallantsails. Two or three boats came alongside. I have had bad gripes for the last day or two.

Friday December 11.   Weighed anchor at 6 a.m. and reached within four miles of our anchorage, when we had to bring up for the tide. We furled the sails at 4 p.m. and Tom and I stowed the mizen topgallantsail. The land seems more fertile than at Hong Kong, and the people look more like Christians. I have been along with the steward and we had a shoulder of mutton for dinner, the finest I have ever tasted.

Saturday December 12.   Anchor up at 8 a.m. and we reached Shanghai about noon and brought up with both anchors not far off shore. Tom and I had a hard job to clean the brass as it had been left two or three days. The carpenter has been very gobby,* but I did not care what he said.

Sunday December 13.   Tom and I have been on shore this afternoon, and it seems to be a very dirty hole, but we did not get as far as the city. There is a vast of beggars, and we saw one juggler doing some wonderful conjuring.

Monday December 14.   Discharging cargo; we have taken a vast of boxes out and a few bags of rice.

Tuesday December 15.   An abominable mizzling day, and we have been working all the time. The steward made us a nice beef steak pie.

Wednesday December 16.   I have been starved with cold† nearly all

*Saucy, insulting.
†In the North of England starve is often used of cold, not hunger.

day sitting keeping tally; a very cold job here. Brown got his discharge for fighting.

Thursday December 17.   We have been feasting on nuts, for many of the boxes were broken. Tom and I have been playing a fine game of cricket on the lower deck.

Friday December 18.   There was a row about the number of bags of rice put into the lighter, and they had to be overhauled, but the mate was right and the Chinaman looked very sheepish for he was frightened he would get a pounding. We had a stylish game of cricket again.

Left: *European factories and Chinese boats.* Below left: *bargemen watching fighting quails on the quay.* Above: *a raree or puppet show: note the drum and cymbals played with the feet.*

Saturday December 19. I bought half a dozen eggs and two loaves; and I ate nearly one loaf and three boiled eggs, and beat one up and put it in my coffee which is as good as milk, and finished the rest of the eggs at tea and part of the second loaf.

Today we have unloaded nothing but rice. Tom and I put some warm water and sugar in our grog and it was very good, and we slept soundly till morning.

Sunday December 20. Tom is reading stories out of the *Edinburgh Journal,* and I can hardly write for him. Nobody got any money last night and so no-one went ashore.

Monday December 21. We are down to the stones.* Tom and I have been oiling the gratings on the poop. I bought a loaf at breakfast time which served for my tea. The *Strathmoor* sailed today with tea for England.

Tuesday December 22. It has been a holiday among the Chinese and there have been no lighters alongside. The others were scrubbing paintwork, and I have been along with the steward.

Wednesday December 23. Tom and I have been oiling the front of the poop and the house; very cold work for it is nearly freezing.

Thursday December 24. We got the stones out just before dark, and

*Probably ballast.

The Dragon Boat Festival on the fifth day of the fifth moon (usually falling in June). Right: *an itinerant doctor.*

then I prepared the plum pudding; afterwards Tom and I got our grog and made a hot punch and it went down very nicely. The crew have been kicking up a fine shanty, singing and dancing fit to stove the decks in. I bought two loaves and half a dozen eggs this morning and cheated him out of one loaf and 6 eggs at night.

Friday December 25. I turned out about 7 a.m. and put the plum pudding in the copper at 8 a.m. It seemed a long time till it was ready. We had a leg of mutton, boiled and sweet potatoes; the plums were a hollering arter each other for they were not sweet enough; but we made a rattling dinner and then Tom and I went on shore without leave or licence. I got a dollar this morning.

Saturday December 26. A barque came in yesterday and hove up alongside for us to take her ballast of great stones. A winch handle rapped me on the head.

Sunday December 27. A cold, uncomfortable day and we have been in bed most of the time. I had both the canaries out of the cage, but the hen seemed frightened. I ate some dates, a loaf and six eggs.

Monday December 28. The monkey had a narrow escape today. He went on board the barque and fell out of her hawsepipe and was a long way astern before he was picked up. I had a hard day's work holding on the winch.

Tuesday December 29. We had a large party today of one lady and

a kid, and about half a dozen captains. I was cuddy* servant, but did not get such a feed as I reckoned on; and to finish off they had tea and the best china of course, and the steward slipped when he was coming from the galley with the teapot in his hand and away goes the lid and knocks off the little knob, which put him in a passion.

Wednesday December 30. Ever so many bags of rice came back which kept them at work till dark. I have been with the steward but had very little to do. The *Antagonist* came in yesterday.

Thursday December 31. We have been unloading sugar till dark, and after tea I made a plum duff for tomorrow. The steward gave me a little sugar, but it was not nearly enough to make it nice, and I added about half a pound which I stole from the hold. The carpenter has gone into the cabin and stolen a lot of grog which made him rather foolish. I got the good news for certain that we are going to London with tea.

There was a fine noise till morning, firing guns and setting off fireworks.

JANUARY 1858

Friday January 1. The second mate, Tom and I have been filling rice bags.

Our plum pudding was very good, and I made a seed cake for tea, but I could not eat any for I had eaten too much duff. We had a

*Cuddy: a small cabin used as a pantry.

Loading tea inland for shipment to the coast. Right: *a Chinese shopping quarter.*

holiday this afternoon, but it rained all the time which was very uncomfortable.

Saturday January 2.   The mate says we are going to Australia instead of England which is not pleasant news. Jim Morrow has been on board today and I had a bit crack* with him. He is in the *Britannia;* she is nearly in load for England. We have very little work. One of the men caught cold and had to be bled.

Sunday January 3.   I bought two bamboo ornaments and stole a carved orange, they cost half-a-dollar. The weather has been nasty and we had a sea-pie that would have been better without sweet potatoes.

Monday January 4.   We have been clearing for tea and took on 100 boxes. The carpenter dropped one and it broke.

Tuesday January 5.   We emptied all the wood out and put 612 chests of tea in. Raining all day, but we spread an awning to keep the tea dry.

Wednesday January 6.   I wrote a letter home but so scrudged up that I made a mess of it. We loaded 270 chests of finest gunpowder tea, 8 of extra fine, and 63 bales of silk and wool. We cleared the cables and hoisted up all the studdingsail booms.

*A talk.

Thursday January 7. We started painting and hoisted the three royal yards aloft. There were 317 chests of fine Congou tea, and I persuaded one of the merchants to sell me one. Tom and I have had a claggum-joying* with stolen sugar.

Friday January 8. A nasty day and very little painting. There were 340 boxes of fine young Hysson, 430 of fine Congou, 45 extra curious fine gunpowder, and 15 bales of wood and silk.

Saturday January 9. A fine day and painting all round, but Tom and I have had little to do.

Sunday January 10. I have been darning stockings but made a poor fist of one that had the heel out. It has rained all day and no bum-boats came down to us. A steamboat came up with a pirate† that she took among the islands.

Monday January 11. Raining hard and we did not turn to until 8 a.m. I made some very good sugar cakes after tea, but we soon polished the lot.

Tuesday January 12. I have been a tinker all afternoon mending a lamp for the steward, and putting a new rivet into the boatswain's knife. We unbent the foresail, mailsail and two topsails.

---

*Claggum is Northumbrian dialect for a sticky toffee; hence claggum-joying: 'mucking about in a sticky mess'.

†Each year a few vessels disappeared in suspicious circumstances, but in 1849 no less than seven opium clippers went missing, probably the victims of pirates. They were the *Anna Eliza, Coquette, Don Juan, Greyhound, Kelpie, Mischief,* and the famous *Sylph.* The brig *Grace Darling,* and the schooner *Amoy Packet,* were also lost at a time when no storms were reported.

Kite flying on a public holiday.

Wednesday January 13. I have been painting all day, a very cold job for there has been a hard frost. The cook and the steward had a row and the cook asked for his discharge and got it; very good, for he was a dirty old man! I filled the kettles after tea.

Thursday January 14. A Dutchman come on board and I think he will ship as cook. The steward kicked the carpenter out of the galley and they were going to fight, but the mate stopped them. I made a stylish cake for tea and the steward put some preserve on it.

Friday January 15. We had a Yorkshire pudding for dinner in the cabin. I put one of the canaries into a new cage made of two little baskets put together.

Saturday January 16. I cleared the galley and got bushels of clarts* out, and just as I had finished the captain came on board with company to tea and I had to go ashore to get bread and milk. The comprador† gave me a pear.

Sunday January 17. The master gave Tom and me two dollars each and we went on shore ashooting, and had a few cracks at coffins and such like; then went towards the town and fell into a shop, where I swopped the two popguns for a fine box for my mammy. Before I went on shore I bought two jars and two screens.

*Clarty in Northumbrian dialect means sticky, muddy, dirty, etc.
†Overseer of the local servants and staff, employed as agent by European companies.

Monday January 18. I was conscripted out of the galley to go and keep tally of the tea. We loaded 450 boxes of Congou, 428 of gunpowder, and 202 boxes of something about the same weight as tea.

Tuesday January 19. I had a cold job puttying round the stern, hanging on by my eyelids. Our cook has come and I think he is good. The carpenter and the steward had a row, and the former gave the latter a clout in the eye and bunged it up – very good! I changed the hen canary yesterday for some stone curios.

Wednesday January 20. We finished puttying, and loaded 180 boxes of Congou. The other boxes that came yesterday are full of rhubarb. A very hard frost this morning, and as soon as the water was put on the decks it froze.

Thursday January 21. There was a dinner- and a tea-party in the cabin and I had to assist: for which I got a good blow-out on boiled mutton and taties, and for tea a tightner of bread and butter as thick as I could lay it on!

Friday January 22. We bent the royals and topgallantsails; a cold job for it blew very hard.

Saturday January 23. Captain Lewis and his wife and eight-day-old baby who have lost their ship are on board as passengers.

I went forr'd to pumpship* when they were clearing the cables, and the master's sampan was below. The coolie had a pan full of rice for his breakfast: the water floated a great dollop out of the hole and it went into the rice. All the hands laughed but it made him swear!

Sunday January 24. The boatswain had two men from the man-o'-war to see him and they stopped to tea. It has been a very wet day so we stopped in the house and overhauled our curios. I put mine into the little box.

Monday January 25. No work for us. We had a nice skulk down in the forecastle.

Tuesday January 26. Tom has been giving me a lesson in the art of boxing. An opium store was burnt to the ground last night. The steward got drunk and because company came he knocked off.

Wednesday January 27. I had to go to the screw ship *Tynemouth*† with two barrels of pork. She is an ugly beast. Our passenger got a ship and has left us. We took on 1,100 chests of Congou.

Thursday January 28. We bent the new sails but had a hard job to stow them. There were 14 bags of bread and 8 chests of tea.

Friday January 29. Very little work today; mostly bending the flying jib and main topgallant staysail. All the ships had their flags half-mast

---

*Sailor's term for using the lavatory or 'heads'.

†The *Tynemouth* was an iron screw-barque of 1,364 tons, built at Newcastle in 1854 for W. Lindsay. She was 238 feet long, 34.5 feet wide, and 18.6 feet deep. She was surveyed in Sunderland and registered in London. Her master in 1858 was Underwood.

An opium shop.

high for a doctor that kicked the bucket. The *Eliza* and *Estha* sailed today.

Saturday January 30.   Raining nearly all day so no work; just what I like.

Sunday January 31.   Tom and I went on shore with the steward, but had no money to spend.

FEBRUARY

Monday February 1.   The sails are loose to dry, and we set up the martingale back-ropes. 325 chests of Congou came today.

Tuesday February 2.   A strong wind all day, but it dropped away towards night. We loaded 440 chests of gunpowder and 285 of Hyson.

Wednesday February 3.   Plenty of tea today; 1,610 boxes of Congou, every one with the ship's name on, which kept me busy.

Friday February 5.   There were 820 chests of Congou yesterday, and 620 today.

Saturday February 6.   Only 300 chests today; it is raining hard and I'm going to bed.

Sunday February 7.   The carpenter has been in bed the last three days just to get clear of work, and the door has been shut all the time. Tom and I think it isn't healthy and we intend to sleep outside. It rained all day.

Monday February 8. It was too cold, so we turned in about twelve and left the door open. The carpenter found out about two hours later and he offered up some prayers for us which would have done your ears good to hear. We took in 270 chests of Congou, and 51 of some funny name that I can't think on, which filled us up, cabin and all. We have six dozen fowls.

Tuesday February 9. It has been raining all day. I set a trap for sparrows before dinner and caught one, so the monkey got it. Four sheep arrived and a lot of straw for them to eat. The captain came on board about 6 p.m. and set us to get one anchor up to be ready for the morning.

Wednesday February 10. The steamboat came alongside at 7 a.m. and we got the anchor up about 9 a.m. He towed us a little below Wousong, where we brought up about half-past eleven. This has been the finest day since we left Hong Kong.

Thursday February 11. Under weigh about 6 a.m. but it came on thick and drizzly, so we brought up shortly after breakfast. Just as dinner was ready we hove up again with a nice wind and sailed away. The pilot left at 3 p.m. and went to a Dutchman wanting a pilot up.

Friday February 12. Last night was our eight hours on deck and before daylight we rigged the booms, and set all the studdingsails on the starboard side before breakfast. We are having pork and peas for a treat.

Saturday February 13. Still a fine strong breeze and we are going as fast as we can to warm weather. The boatswain was over greedy for work in harbour and has none for us now.

Sunday February 14. We set the starboard main topmast studding-sail first thing this morning, and in the afternoon set them all on the port side, then in the dog watch* took the starboard ones down, and set them again between eight and twelve. We had a sea-pie for dinner.

Monday February 15. A delightful day and I let the pigeons adrift.

Tuesday February 16. We took all the starboard studdingsails down last night. Two of the pigeons flew overboard and there was overmuch wind for them to get up again so that is two less of the family.

Wednesday February 17. Helman and I have been giving the poop a coat of varnish-oil and white paint mixed together.† It has been pretty warm today.

Thursday February 18. We set the starboard studdingsails first thing this morning, and washed decks as usual. We gave the main deck a lacquering of varnish after dinner (a sea-pie).

Friday February 19. Squally with rain and we furled the mizen

*The dog watches are from 4 to 6 p.m. and 6 to 8 p.m., the other watches being four hours long: they allow the times when a man is on watch to be varied from day to day.
†Note the white poop on the illustration of the *Vanguard*.

topgallantsail and royal. I split my breeches' backside and had a tight job at them after dinner. There is a heavy sea running and she is rolling the water on the decks. We have taken in the starboard lower and topmast studdingsails.

Saturday February 20. We took in all the topgallant stunsails last night, but carried away our fore topmast studdingsail boom about 4.30 a.m. through carelessness; we soon rigged another and set the sails, then royals and mizen topgallantsail; and shortly after set the flying jib and main topgallant staysail. Took in the studdingsails and all the little sails but the main topgallantsail. We passed many tree roots.

Sunday February 21. First thing this morning we set the port studdingsails and took them in before dinner as it looked squally. About 4 p.m. a squall caught us on the starboard side and we had to take in all sail but close reefed topsails. It did not last long, and by 8 p.m. we had all set again except the royals.

Monday February 22. The weather is more settled, and we set the royals and starboard main topgallant and fore topmast and lower studdingsails. We passed Direction Island about noon and crossed the line at 5 p.m.

Tuesday February 23. There is nothing to do but trim the yards a little for we are in a dangerous place. We passed a ship at anchor, and we had to remain above this dog watch.

Wednesday February 24. We set the royals before breakfast, and after it all the studdingsails but the lower on the starboard side, and the port main topgallant studdingsail. We are in company with two ships, one a Spaniard. Our curiosity was raised about something that looked like a boat under sail, but when we came up to it found it was only a bundle of roots.

Thursday February 25. We came into the Straits of Sunday, and a boat came alongside with several monkeys; the master bought taties and fruit, some male monkeys and various other things.

In the afternoon some canoes came alongside with shells and coral, but I was in my bunk and knew nothing about it, and am very vexed with Tom for not calling me up. John Tom stole a cage full of Java sparrows from the first boat.

Friday February 26. About 5 a.m. we set all the studdingsails on the port side and took both anchors in and put them on the maindeck. A booby settled beside the man at the wheel and he caught it.

Saturday February 27. Last night they took in the studdingsails. We put the cables below, and the cook killed a sheep.

Sunday February 28. We took the royals in last night and set them again this morning; after tea it was squally, so we stowed them. We had sea-pie, roast mutton and roast potatoes for dinner. Potter caught a booby and Philip twisted its neck.

MARCH

Monday March 1. Potter caught two more boobies last night and let one away today. A squall took us aback* at 3 a.m., and it teemed down by bucketfuls till we went below. Our starboard fore topsail halliards broke again just before breakfast. It rained all morning and we tacked ship at noon.

Tuesday March 2. A heavy squall last night and we had to reef the topsails and set them as soon as the watch was called; also the topgallantsails. We set the studdingsails on the starboard side before dinner.

Wednesday March 3. The wind is right aft and we have the studdingsails set on both sides, and all the fore-and-aft sails stowed. Last night the booby catcher caught two sitting close together on the mizen royal yard. We had fried eggs for tea and I think they would do us no harm every night!

Thursday March 4. We took in all the starboard studdingsails and set the port main topmast studdingsails. I think they will stand for a long time as we are in the SE Trades.

Friday March 5. Our lower studdingsails are shape (1), and the master wants to lose no time and he bent a fore topmast staysail to make it into a square (2).

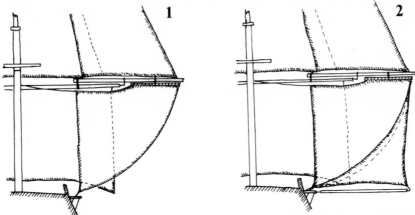

Saturday March 6. We took in the patent,† and set without it last night at 8 p.m. This fine breeze will soon fetch us home.

Sunday March 7. All I have done today is open five cocoanuts and they were bad except the last. The cook killed a sheep yesterday and we polished his bones today. There was a splendid monkey fight between the celebrated coves, Vicious Muggins, Tim Gentle, and Old Tarry Jack, the two latter against the former.

*I.e. a sudden shift of wind blew the sails back against the masts.

† The extra studdingsail mentioned above.

Monday March 8. We set the big studdingsail this morning, and I had a splendid dinner of roast leg of mutton and potatoes, which will have to serve me until next week.

Tuesday March 9. The weather is still fine, but I have a nasty toothache. We came up with a vessel upon our port bow. James O'Heggarty fell headforemost from the mizen topsail yard into the top. I asked him what made him come down, and he said: 'Common Sense.' I swapped a guernsey for a pair of sea boots.

Wednesday March 10. Calm all day; a ship came in sight astern so the master ordered 30 fathoms of chain to be taken out of the trunk and put down in the forecastle, and we soon left her behind for it made us sail faster.

Thursday March 11. We set the starboard main topgallantsail last night, and this morning set the main and lower studdingsails. We have been setting up the backstays fore and aft.

Friday March 12. This is my birthday, but I am going to keep it on Sunday when we will have something to scoff.

Saturday March 13. Killed a sheep and I got the blather. There is only one left and she is going blaring about the decks in a pitiful manner.

Sunday March 14. Tom and I had a few nice glasses of wine with warm water and sugar. The cook made some sweet cakes for tea, but when they were opened they were as sad as a fosy turnip.

Monday March 15. Three of us have been knocking the rust off the ironwork and painting it red;* all the rest were setting up the main and mizen topmast rigging.

Tuesday March 16. I have been at the same work, and the rest have finished the main topmast rigging. I broke the little blade of my knife. The carpenter started making a lower yard.

Wednesday March 17. Set the fore topmast rigging up and finished all the red paint.

Thursday March 18. Our starboard topgallant studdingsail tack block took it into its head to have a run down to the poop to see what it felt like there.

Friday March 19. We took in the big 'un,† and set the little 'un last night, and took in the little 'un, and set the big 'un this morning.

Saturday March 20. The last sheep was killed and there were three little ones in her. We passed a large ship called the *Backworth* at 2 p.m.

Sunday March 21. Sea-pie as usual and I filled my belly. The cook caught a large flying fish and he is going to cure it for me.**

---

*Chipping rust and painting with red lead: a never-ending job on any ship.
†The mainsail.
**There are two dried rays of a flying fish stuck into the diary.

Monday March 22. We shifted the big studdingsail over to the starboard side. This is the steward's thirty-second birthday.

Tuesday March 23. It began to blow last night and we took in all the small sails and single reefed the topsails, but it moderated towards midnight, and we set them all again, and a topmast studdingsail. We were given a glass of grog and went to bed.

Thursday March 25. The wind is very light and shifting about. All the studdingsails are set on the port side.

Friday March 26. The wind shifted to the starboard quarter and we had to take in the port studdingsails. The fore rigging was set up this morning. The master set O'Heggarty and me to sluice the poop down.

Saturday March 27. A brig came towards us, and the boatswain was bending on the ensign, but just as he hoisted it clear of the boom end, the bend slipped and it went flying away so that he had to go out to the gaff end (which is a notable feat) to get it in again; if it had been anybody else the master would have kicked him off the poop, for when the brig hoisted her's, it was the St George, showing her to be a man-of-war; then she hoisted her name, the *Percian*.

The wind shifted to the NW and we had to tack at 2 p.m. We passed three ships going the same way as us, and exchanged signals with two. It blew hard towards night, and we took in all the small sails and single reefed the topsails.

Sunday March 28. It blew hard last night and we had to take in all the sails, but close reefed topsails. We set the courses* reefed this morning, and just before dark stowed everything but the fore and main topsails. When at dinner Tailor's monkey got at his canary and ate it tail feathers and all.

Monday March 29. The wind moderated this morning and we set the courses, and unrolled a little of the topsails and set the fore and main topgallantsails. Towards night it blew hard again, and we stowed all but the three close reefed topsails, and then slewed her round. We sighted land this morning. Passed the *Wandering Jew* last night taking her rest without any sails set.

Tuesday March 30. We set all sail by degrees but the single reefed topsails, and stowed the royals and mizen topgallantsail at 6 p.m. The boatswain says we will have a fair wind tomorrow.

Wednesday March 31. We set all sail this morning, and according to the boatswain's prophecy, in the afternoon there was a fair wind and we set all the studdingsails on the port side. We set the main rigging up.

APRIL

Thursday April 1. Like a great gouk I lost my best cap overboard. The wind drew round to the starboard side and we had to shift the

*The foresail and mainsail.

big studdingsail over. We have taken in all the studdingsails and braced up the yards. Last night in the first watch we passed the Cape.*

Saturday April 3. She broke off about 7 a.m. and we put her about at 8 a.m., and shortly afterwards set all the studdingsails on the port side.

Sunday April 4. The wind drew right aft and we set the starboard main topmast and topgallantsails. We exchanged signals with a little Dutch barque. At 8 p.m. we set the starboard studdingsail.

Monday April 5. We unbent the foresail, fore topsail, and bent the old ones. Cleared everything out from under the topgallant forecastle.

Tuesday April 6. We knocked the rust off the anchors and polished the cables. I have been making putty out of paint oil and whiting.

Wednesday April 7. We unbent the mainsail and bent the old one first thing this morning; all hands were set to tar her down.

Friday April 9. We sent the fore topgallantsail and royal down, and gave them a little repairing, and sent them up again.

Saturday April 10. Finished all the tarring, and started scraping where needed.

Sunday April 11. We sighted St Helena about 2 p.m. and came up just at dark so we did not see it very well. An American whaler crossed our bows just before we passed the island.

Tuesday April 13. I have been mixing paint all day and the rest have been putting it on.

Wednesday April 14. We have been at the same work.

Thursday April 15. Very little work going on and I had nothing to do. All the painting on the maindeck is finished.

Friday April 16. We passed Ascension last night, but did not see it.

Saturday April 17. No work except washing the decks as usual.

Sunday April 18. I had all my curios out and they are in good order. Tom and I were invited to dinner and I had one wing and a leg of fowl, one piece of mutton pie – A1 – and taties, also one piece of plum duff, a glass of wine, and bread and cheese. We are in latitude 2° 32′ s. I had a bath yesterday morning, and will have one every other morning as long as the weather is fine.

Monday April 19. We crossed the line about 2 p.m. The lower studdingsail halliards carried away last night. We have bent the old main topsail and fore topmast staysail.

Tuesday April 20. We lost the SE Trades in 1° 18′ N and had some scull-dragging at the yards. We have been trying to catch a shark but he had no notion. The steward served out lime juice.

Wednesday April 21. Plenty of rain last night, and plenty of pull and hauling. We have been scraping the sun rails.

Thursday April 22. It rained very hard this morning, and we filled the four water casks. I think we are in the NE Trades.

*The Cape of Good Hope.

Saturday April 24.   An outward bounder passed us last evening. There has been plenty of lightning and wind. I made a syringe to shoot water at the monkeys.

Sunday April 25.   I took my bed out on the forecastle and spread the quilt over us to keep off the sun, and Tom and I lay there all day.

Monday April 26.   The steward and I cleaned the mate's berth out, while the lads scraped the masts.

Tuesday April 27.   I have had a large wash, the last till home. We've varnished the masts.

Wednesday April 28.   We put preventer braces on the fore and main topsail yards, and painted the mastheads and tops white.

Thursday April 29.   A fair wind last night. All hands scrubbing and scraping.

Friday April 30.   We scrubbed the house and oiled it, and also the gratings on the poop. Set the fore and main topmast studdingsails and topgallant studdingsails, and pulled them down at 8 p.m.

MAY

Sunday May 2.   Just as all other Sundays. Tom and I set a bottle adrift with a letter in it for fun.

Monday May 3.   A change of wind, but not for long.

Tuesday May 4.   Painted the poop and scraped the ladders. There is a vast amount of seaweed floating past. We have had a fore topmast studdingsail set this afternoon till about 6 p.m.

Wednesday May 5.   Painting and oiling. We set the fore and main topmast and topgallantsails.

Thursday May 6.   Took in the studdingsails last night. It has been calm all day, and about 6 p.m. we caught a fine dolphin. I have had a headache since Monday, but it is rather bad tonight.

Friday May 7.   We had dolphin for breakfast, very good. There is little work to do as she is nearly clean.

Saturday May 8.   The cook killed a pig after dinner, and I had part of his tripe boiled for tea which was very, very nice.

Sunday May 9.   We had fried pork for breakfast; a roast leg for dinner; and cut slices warmed with fried dough for tea.

Monday May 10.   Light winds. We exchanged signals with a barque bound for Liverpool called the *Gondola*.

The captain has been amusing himself fishing for monkeys with a line from the poop onto the house baited with pork skin; he also had Janey Taylor* tied to the logline to see how many knots she could do along the decks.

*Another of the monkeys.

Tuesday May 11. Scrubbed and varnished the maindeck. We exchanged signals with a Dutchman from Batavia, and at 8 p.m. set off a blue light. She returned it. We set the fore topmast studdingsail at 5 a.m. Light daffing winds all day.

Wednesday May 12. Set the fore and main topgallant studdingsails last night, and today set the lower and main topmast stunsails. We had a nice breeze last night, but it has been calm all day.

Thursday May 14. Took in the studdingsails at 5 a.m. and braced the yards sharp up. A fair wind about noon, and we set the port studdingsails again.

Saturday May 15. A fine breeze last night which increased through the day. We have been cleaning the poop.

Sunday May 16. A splendid breeze right aft, and if it continues I hope to be home in a fortnight. We were making from 11 to 12 knots last night.

Monday May 17. We took in all the studdingsails last night, but the fore topmast and lower. Towards daylight we set them again and have had light winds all day.

Tuesday May 18. We hauled the yards for'd, and took in all the port studdingsails. We exchanged signals with a French barque, the *Julious* from the West Indies. The wind increased towards night and we took in the fore and main topgallant and topmast studdingsails, and mizen topgallantsail and royal, and the main and fore royals. We were 720 miles from the Lizard light at noon.

Wednesday May 19. Shortened sail last night, and set them as usual at daybreak. It was rather cloudy today, and they did not get the sun at noon.*

Thursday May 20. We put the port anchor on the bow, and about 30 fathoms of cable and 18 on the starboard side. A thick haze all day, and we took in the studdingsails, except for the lower, the royals and mizen topgallantsail.

Friday May 21. Killed the last pig. We set all sail as usual.

Saturday May 22. Abreast of the Lizard at 5 a.m., but did not sight it, and at 7 p.m. sighted the Isle of Wight. A pilot cutter tried to come up to us, but he had to give up the chase. Overhauled seven fathoms range on each cable. We had roast pork and duff for dinner.

Sunday May 23. I was going to send a letter but the boat left before I finished it. We have a steamboat and a pilot, but the boat will not take hold till we reach the Downs, for there is a fine breeze.

The final stroke of this journal of the principal events that occurred to the British ship *Vanguard* and her crew from England to China and back is that Tom and I inverted the last of our last bottle, kept for the occasion.

*For a sextant reading.

Clipper
to Adelaide

1862

Edward Lacey

In the early 1850s South Australia developed an extensive wool trade with England in exchange for general cargoes from London. Most of this business was in the hands of three firms: Orient, Devitt & Moore, and Elder. The first of these was started by James Thompson, who had a number of small ships trading to the West Indies. His first vessel on the Australian run was the Orient *(who gave her name to the line), built in 1853 in the Nelson Docks, Rotherhithe, to designs of Mr Bilbe.*

Later Mr James Anderson joined the firm of James Thompson & Co., and eventually became the senior partner, when the firm's name was changed to Anderson, Anderson & Co. The Orient Line of clippers were the forerunners of the Orient Line of steamers, later the P & O and Orient.

Apart from Dutton's lithograph the editor has been unable to obtain illustrations of the Orient. *Fortunately the Sunderland Art Gallery and Museum has a few photographs of the* Torrens *taken in 1892 on a voyage to Australia. She was the last composite ship to be built (1875), and her general layout was similar to that of the* Orient. *These photographs, reproduced through the courtesy of the Director and Trustees of the museum, have been used to illustrate events described by Mr Lacey. They have additional importance as being taken when Joseph Conrad was a member of the crew of the* Torrens, *and he appears in one of them.*

The Orient, *International Number 12981, Code Letters LFCK, was a ship of 1,032 gross tonnage. Length 190 feet, breadth 35.5 feet,* depth 21.4 feet. She was built by Bilbe in 1853 in twelve months in London, where she was surveyed and registered. Bilbe's ships were noted for being fast and wet.

In 1879 the Orient was sold to Cox Bros. of Waterford, and she was still afloat in 1925 as a coal-hulk at Gibraltar, and then was sold for breaking up. The butt of her figurehead was obtained by the Orient Line, and is now in the firm's possession. On the 1st of May, 1960, there was a merger between the P & O and Orient Lines; which are now known as the P & O Orient.

This account of the voyage of the Orient from London to Adelaide in 1862 was written by Mr Edward Lacey (possibly Facey, or Tacey – the handwriting is difficult to decipher), and was among the effects of Mr William Hewitt, of Gosforth, Northumberland. Nothing is known of how it came into his possession. The handwriting in the original manuscript varies greatly with the weather in which it was written; during storms it is barely legible.

See Appendix B for further details of the Orient's sailings.

The ship Orient passing Gibraltar on her maiden voyage carrying troops to the Crimea in 1854. Lithograph by T. G. Dutton, a marine artist whose output of portraits of men-of-war, merchant sailing ships, steamships and yachts was prodigious. The commercial production of lithographic marine prints ceased with his death in 1882, and was replaced by photography.

Gravesend.

On board the Orient, *off the Nore, May 28th, 1862, London*
Wednesday May 28. I came on board at 11 a.m., and we ran out of
Shadwell Basin at 3 p.m., saw the last of my father standing on
Shadwell Pier. We had a good run down the Thames, and the captain
and Channel pilot joined us at Gravesend. At 7 p.m. reached the Nore,
where the crew were put into action by the first mate yelling: 'Clear
away the cables boys, and let go the anchor!' We will ride at anchor
until morning when we expect to run out with the tide. Four bells*
(10 p.m.) has just sounded and I must turn into my bunk for the first
time.

Thursday May 29. Slept very uncomfortably last night, owing to new
quarters and thinking all night of home and friends whom I may never
see again. Awoke about 5 a.m. by hearing 20 to 30 men singing in a
cheerful tone, 'I am off to Charles Town'; tumbled out and went on
deck to find the crew were weighing anchor.

When the anchor was up the steam tug took us in tow and threaded

---

*Time is marked on board ship by striking a bell at half-hour intervals in
watches of four hours: e.g. in the afternoon watch one bell is sounded at
12.30 p.m., two bells at 1, three bells at 1.30, and so on until eight bells at 4
p.m. The sequence is repeated every four hours day and night except in the
dog watches from 4 to 8 p.m. The first dog watch ends at four bells (6 p.m.),
the last dog watch is then sounded as one bell for 6.30, two bells at 7.00,
three bells at 7.30, reverting to eight bells at 8 p.m. On some ships 'Little one
bell' was sounded – a light stroke five minutes after the start of a night watch
to call a muster of the men.

Top: *wrecks ashore near Margate.* Above: *passengers on board the* Torrens *in* 1892 *(Sunderland Art Gallery).*

her way out to sea in an almost incredible manner. There is a nice breeze springing up and the good ship is trying to jump ahead of the tug, and seems to be revelling in her own element. I am ready for breakfast, and had better go and see what's to be had.

The entrance to Plymouth harbour.

9 p.m. Very dirty weather, cold wind and rain all day. We sighted a wreck off the Goodwin Sands. All the passengers were sick; we passed the Isle of Wight about midday.

Friday May 30. Cold wind and rain, and any amount of sickness on board.

Saturday May 31. Turned out at 6 a.m. and walked the poop for two hours before breakfast. A fine day and we met several homeward bound vessels; our first Saturday night at sea. We are now on the Devonshire coast about 14 miles from the land. The passengers and crew are on deck watching the sun go down, making a superb panorama view, while the ship is gliding along at 8 knots like a swan without any perceptible movement. The water is smooth and the sun setting behind the hills looks like a sheet of gold. It is a magnificent sight, as if England knew we were taking our last look at her and wished to display herself in all her glory. Night has now hidden her from our view. We heave a deep sigh and go below to think of those we are leaving behind. *Sic transit gloria Mundi.*

JUNE

Sunday June 1. When I went on deck this morning we were in sight of Plymouth, and ran into the Sound about 9 a.m. and dropped anchor a mile and a half from shore. It is a splendid morning and I

Plymouth.

think Plymouth from the sea is the prettiest landscape in England. The town lies ahead protected from the sea by high cliffs and flanked with strong fortifications and batteries. Devonport is two miles to the left, and on the right are strong fortifications being built to command the entrance to the Sound. Soon after our arrival we were boarded by Customs House Officers and other officials. Great excitement on the arrival of letters for passengers. After dinner some of us engaged a boat and went on shore. Visited some of the churches, most of the principal buildings, had tea and then returned at 7 p.m. Tumbled below, wrote my last letters for home and turned in.

Monday June 2. A fine morning with all hands busy preparing for sea. Fowls, cattle and all kinds of provisions are coming on board. After breakfast we made up another shore party and purchased a few articles we required, returning to the vessel at 11 a.m.

I sealed up my letters and placed them on the cuddy table ready for the pilot to take ashore with him. The last moments have now arrived, the word is given, 'Weigh anchor' when a cry is heard, 'Boat alongside!' It was the agent with more letters. I made a frantic rush to the gangway and watched the first mate sort the mail. Presently he cried out, 'Three letters for Mr Lacey', whereupon that individual immediately seized the letters and dived below to read them; having spent some time in reading them over and over again, when I went on deck the *Orient* was on the move. 'Heave away my lads – heave away!'

The anchor rose slowly from the muddy bed and our ship creaked and groaned as our powerful friend in front, vomiting volumes of smoke and dirt, slowly drew us toward the entrance of the Plymouth Breakwater. The few friends on board began to crowd the gangway, to bid adieu. There was a dull, heavy splash as the towline was loosed, and the steamer turned her head toward the land, stopping a moment alongside us to pick up the shore friends who stood uncovered to receive with sorrow the cheers of all on board; for many it will be a last farewell. The wind filled our sails and the *Orient* moved on her way.

10 p.m. Plymouth is nowhere in view; I can just discern land on the weather bow, but darkness is falling fast, so I will say goodbye to my motherland and trust we may have a happy voyage, and a speedy arrival at our destination; may every success attend those of us seeking fame and fortune in the distant country; and a happy return to Old England.

Tuesday June 3. A fine day. Put my cabin in trim and made everything fast and shipshape order. At 4 p.m. we sighted the Eddystone Lighthouse. Running 10 knots all day, close hauled.

Wednesday June 4. Arrived at the Lizard at 6 a.m., and by noon the land was out of sight. The deck was crowded with passengers and crew to take a last look at Old England. We are now out on the broad Atlantic, and passed several ships outward bound. Dull and misty.

The Eddystone Lighthouse.

As slow our ship her foaming track
  Against the wind was cleaving;
Her trembling pennant still looked back
  To that dear Isle 'twas leaving;
So loath we part from all we love,
  From all the links that bind us;
So turn our hearts as on we roamed,
  To those we've left behind us.
June 4th, '62

Thursday June 5.   Cold and misty with rain, heavy seas and head winds. All the passengers are sick. At 11 a.m. spoke to a French brig and gave her three British cheers.

Friday June 6.   Sea rough, head winds, ship close hauled, and about ship every four hours.

Saturday June 7.   Wind still ahead and squally with rain. We are now skirting the Bay of Biscay and expect to have a rough time of it.

Sunday June 8.   The weather is fearfully rough* and the wind dead against us and blowing big guns. The ship is rolling and pitching like a tub on the water and the sea is flying over the decks and carrying everything before it. Three windows of the stern cabin were washed in, and the place filled with water; pumps were rigged to clear the cabin. If this is the Bay of Biscay, I don't care how soon we are out of it! Church Service was held at 10 a.m.

Monday June 9.   The wind still ahead and the ship close hauled; the sea is running mountains high. When the *Orient* lay in London Docks I little thought spray would fly over the main yard-arm, but now I am beginning to learn the power of the Atlantic. Several ships in sight, and high land Cape Finisterre bearing SE by S. A squally night.

Tuesday June 10.   Still bucking about the Bay of Biscay; no sleep last night as the wind was dead against us and very rough indeed; I was pitched out of my bunk three times. It is still blowing hard.

Wednesday June 11.   A fine day but windy and set against us. We are not running more than three knots. Cleared the Bay about dinner time. The sea is turbulent and the night squally.

Thursday June 12.   The wind is still ahead of us and beating a heavy sea. The day is fine and at 2 p.m. we sighted the Portuguese coast on our lee bow, eighty miles off.

---

*The skippers of the little Adelaide clippers made light of weather that would have scared the commanders of vessels three times their size; and the South Australian traders prided themselves on carrying a main topgallantsail when other ships were under reefed topsails; but their decks were habitually wet, and when running down the easting they were swept from end to end by every roaring sea, and even in a fresh breeze their decks were hidden in spray.

The Torrens *on a voyage to Australia.* (*Sunderland Art Gallery*).

Friday June 13.   A fair wind and skimming along beautifully at 12 knots.

Soon after leaving Plymouth it was discovered that the supply of flour put on board in London by some oversight was very small and fast disappearing. While debating the matter the man at the masthead cried out: 'Sail on the weather bow!' The captain came on deck to examine her and she turned out to be a Dutchman. All hands were sent aloft to make sail and run up to the stranger. When near enough our skipper signalled her for flour (we had been on short allowance since leaving land). After a series of signals we hove to and our first mate put off in a boat for the Dutch barque, and soon returned with a good stock of flour. Brava, Dutchman – she was bound from Sunderland to Shanghai with coal, but had met rough weather in which she lost her bowsprit, and had to put into Dieppe. The captain was a gallant fellow and sent very courteous messages to our ladies. After returning salutes we both set sail and soon lost sight of each other.

Saturday June 14.   The weather is getting very warm. We are now shaking down into a settled mode of existence. Our ladies are appearing regularly every morning on the poop, and their fair countenances are one by one illuminating the cuddy table.

Sayings and doings on a ship are more interesting to friends at

119

home than to those on board. Being so long without change, our amusements grow stale and insipid; though the never failing cards, chess, backgammon, and draughts serve to while away many a weary hour. Squaills,* in which the ladies join and are becoming dangerous rivals for the gentlemen, has a large patronage; the piano is well used and as several of our gents are proficient in singing and the stack of music on board is large, the tunes of 'Aunt Sally' and 'In the Strand' are often heard. Gymnastics are also in vogue, the ship and her rigging affording ample space and opportunity; reading, eating, and sleeping conclude our occupations. I was taken ill tonight owing to the sudden change in climate.

Sunday June 15. The hot weather is setting in fast. I was very ill in the night with diarrhoea and fainting fits. Doctor Nash was called and sat with me all night. He was very kind, but this morning I am low and weak and cannot leave my bunk.

At 10 a.m. Divine Service was held on the poop and the Reverend Thomas Field, a fellow passenger, preached an impressive sermon. He visited me in my cabin after the service, as I was not able to attend church.

7 p.m. The coast of Madeira is twenty miles on our lee bow.

Monday June 16. The weather is getting hotter; the wind is aft and we are running at 10 knots. I remain ill and have not taken food for twenty-four hours. The doctor visits me three times a day; he has just ordered the steward to get me some arrowroot. A number of whales have been keeping us company and their frolics amused me as I lay in my bunk watching through the porthole.

Tuesday June 17. Raining hard and a heavy sea beating; it is very close and hot. I had a restless night and am very weak today. Doctor Nash is very attentive to me.

Wednesday June 18. We are now in the tropics and it is fearfully hot. The wind is fair and we are running 8 knots. I had a good night's rest and feel much better. Doctor is giving me port wine and arrowroot, which is better than all his medicines.

Day by day the heat is increasing and interferes with the pleasures of the ladies on the poop. Two subjects are being mooted, viz. an awning to cover the poop, and a shower bath in the morning, which I hope will be carried out, as they will be most agreeable.

Thursday June 19. I feel considerably better this morning and am able to turn out of my bunk. Doctor allowed me on deck for an hour. A fine day but extremely hot; very clear horizon, running 10 knots.

The bath has been constructed and the awning erected. A few

*A table game played with wooden discs in sets of different colours: each player in turn places his discs so that they partly overhang the edge of the table, then strikes them with the palm of the hand towards a lead target in the centre. The principle is similar to the English game of shove-halfpenny.

improvements are required to the bath to make it more private for the ladies, namely a curtain or two, and a slight alteration to the tap which wastes a considerable quantity of water. The bath consists of four pieces of canvas, four feet by nine feet, stitched together at the edges, and stretched top and bottom on a slight frame of wood, the top being covered by a piece of canvas pierced with holes and hung from the poop in front of the cuddy, the side nearest the cuddy being provided with a door. It is fixed in the morning when the decks are washed, and each person is limited to three buckets of water, a quantity agreed to, though in the present heat more would be agreeable. The bath is greatly relished by the ladies who may be seen every morning (I don't say that I see them) as so many editions of 'The Woman in White'.

Friday June 20. A fine day, but dreadfully hot; I am much better and remained on deck all day. About noon our eyes were strained to catch a glimpse of Cape St Antonia, bearing some distance to the sw. However, the distance was too great and there was a little mist, but we all declared that we had seen 'something'.

This afternoon the first mate related to me the particulars of a fire on the last voyage home which all but destroyed our ship and hurried upwards of one hundred souls into eternity; but under Providence and the heroic conduct of officers and crew, all were saved. The first mate kindly lent me the following account from the *Shipping and Mercantile Gazette.*

Monday 4th November 1861 saw the splendid clipper built ship *Orient* leave Adelaide with 70 passengers, a cargo principally of wool and several cases for the Great Exhibition.* A 40-day passage found her at the Cape, where four days were pleasantly spent. On Thursday 2nd January 1862, Latitude 11° 46′ s, Longitude 9° 50′ w about 9 a.m. smoke was seen to issue from the steerage. After a short search the seat of the fire, now visible to everyone, was found to be between decks. The hatchways were then by order of Captain Lawrence, battened down, holes cut in the deck, the hose inserted, and for many and many weary hours did crew and passengers, now divided into regular watches, pump and pump until the joyful news went round that they were gaining on the fire, and here let it be said to the credit of the fair sex on board, that even in the greatest danger, not the slightest panic or confusion was observable amongst them. In fact so far as they were concerned, it would have been difficult to have told that anything unusual was occurring.

In the meantime the boats had been stowed with necessities, and were towing astern; the cutter and lifeboat, however, unfortunately

*The International Exhibition in London, opened May 1st 1862.

fouled and broke adrift. Soon after daylight on the 3rd a sail was observed ahead, before noon the Dutch barque *Cammisara des Flaning vander Flun* [?] was spoken, and informed that the ship was on fire. A few hours after, the ladies, children, and some stores were safely put on board the barque, and on January 5th the two ships in consort anchored in Clarence Bay (Ascension Island), where the friendly services rendered by H.M.S. *Arrogant* and *Maandes* soon made our ship again ready for sea.*

Till 18th January, both passengers and crew enjoyed themselves to their hearts content, and received every kindness on all sides. On that day the ship again set sail and sighted Old England and more on the 21st February; and here let every expression of thankfulness be made to Captain Lawrence, officers, and crew of the *Orient* for their heroic conduct in a time of great danger and distress, which under Providence has been the means of saving the ship.

Saturday June 21. Turned out at 5 a.m. for a shower bath; have been ordered by the doctor to take one every morning. A fine day but the heat is excessive. At noon we sighted a sail on our weather bow; when near enough signalled and found that she was a Sunderland ship bound for Shanghai.

Sunday June 22. Had a shower bath at 5 a.m.; a fine morning but the wind was calm and progress slow. Divine Service was held at 10 a.m. on the poop. Text, 2nd Proverbs, 5th verse. I think there is more solemnity in a church service held on board a ship than in the grandest cathedral.

> We are all on deck together,
>   On the fair sabbath day;
> In the glowing tropic weather,
>   Where we are gathered to pray,
> While our good ship holds
>   On her steadfast way.

At 6 p.m. Service was again held by our respected clergyman. A shoal of flying fish have kept us company.

Monday June 23. A fine day but the wind calm and we make little

---

*Twelve of her timbers had to be replaced, and the planking of the maindeck as far aft as the main hatch. The underwriters presented Captain Lawrence with a piece of plate valued at £100, and £800 for himself, his officers, and his men. The discipline of the passengers and crew were exemplary and undoubtedly saved the ship. (Editor.)

advance. We are now 10° north of the Line. Several porpoises are playing around us and there was great excitement when one of these slimy brutes was harpooned and hauled on board by about twenty tars, and rare fun it was. He measured 13 feet long and weighed 2 hundredweight.

Tuesday June 24. A fine breeze sprang up and we are running at 10 knots. Every little zephyr during the last few days has been hailed as the NE Trades, and there was disappointment upon being informed that they were only the outskirts; however, this morning everybody is pleased to hear that the stiff breeze now blowing really is the Trades, and we look forward to a good week's work.

10 p.m. We have been bowling along at a slapping pace and the ship has proved to the most incredulous that 'she can go' and we have passed everything we have come across. At daylight a number of sails were seen over our bow; mere specks on the horizon, and by nightfall they were spoken to and far out of sight astern. The sky is overcast tonight, and the atmosphere oppressive.

Wednesday June 25. 4 p.m. Sighted another ship bound for Shanghai.

10 p.m. This evening I sat over the stern watching the phosphorus light in the water. The sky was overcast and a SW swell. There is a sail ahead but too dark to signal; we'll talk to her in the morning.

Thursday June 26. Raining hard but no wind. At noon there was a heavy squall and it was dark at 6.30; very hot and oppressive. We are off the African coast and can see flashes of lightning in the desert. At daylight this morning we overhauled the ship we saw last night. She was an English barque, the *Queen Hastens,* from Swansea to Shanghai, 31 days out.

Our first catastrophe occurred this morning. One of our young gentlemen had just taken a bath and proceeded to call a 'lady fair' that all was ready, but instead of walking to her boudoir, he took to leaping. A large cane bottomed chair stood in the way and instead of removing the obstacle, he took a leap. Unfortunately our modern Adonis was not blessed with wings, and cuddies have ceilings with which the head of our too ardent gent came into violent contact, curing his gallantry and confining him to his cabin where the doctor recommended him to seek quiet and rest. The poor fellow earned much sympathy from the ladies; particularly the unwitting cause of our first mishap.

Friday June 27. A fine morning but the ship is like a log in a dead calm. We have left the NE Trades and are now creeping slowly towards the Equator. Last night all were cheered by the sight of the Southern Cross over the bows.

Whilst writing in my log book I was disturbed by a row and racket all along the vessel, and on going up found on the quarter deck, 'all

covered with wounds and glory' a huge shark that had been harpooned by one of the foremast men. Many ladies were on the poop
looking on, but when his jaws began to work they made themselves
scarce; however, the deadly steel soon did its work, and with a
struggle-uggle-uggle the unfortunate denizen of the deep gave up the
ghost. The captain said he had seldom seen so large a brute. The
edible parts are near the tail and taste like rump steak. These were
soon separated from the rest of the oily carcass which was thrown
overboard to make a meal for the first shark that came across it.

This morning I heard the captain say to the mate, 'Look out for a
squall today'. I thought he must be mad, there was not a cloud to be
seen, not a breath of wind, and the sea like a duckpond; but 'sure
enough' as Paddy says, the skipper was correct. At 2 p.m. a breeze
sprang up and the horizon on our weather bow looked dark, and the
sea began to swell and roll. Captain Harris was sent for, who immediately ordered; 'All hands aloft, take in sail and make everything
fast for a flying squall!' They went up like a swarm of monkeys;
presently we heard a distant roar as if a thousand locomotives were
approaching and before the captain's order was accomplished the
squall came upon us with such force that the *Orient* was thrown upon
her side. She recovered herself in a few seconds and trembled from
stem to stern, while her massive masts shook like young saplings.

After the squall had passed I looked at the captain and thought he
was paler than usual; had he seen me no doubt he would have found
the same. I am sure I felt pale enough!

Saturday June 28. A fine morning with a SE wind. Turned out at
4 a.m. and had a shower bath. At 8 a.m. a shoal of flying fish crossed
our bows.

9.30 a.m. All hands on deck to put ship about. *11 a.m.* We were
going along smoothly with all sail set when we were suddenly over-
taken by a squall. At 4 p.m. we were visited by another. I am told
that as we approach the Line we shall encounter a great number of
squalls. We are about 3° 40′ N of the Line and expect to cross it on
Monday. *6 p.m.* It is fearfully hot and I cannot endure it below. *9 p.m.*
The log has just been heaved and we are not doing more than 5 knots.
Midnight. There is no wind and the heat is intense; the passengers
are all sleeping on deck and with the exception of the man at the
wheel, the ship looks as if she had been visited by some plague and
was a phantom vessel gliding on with dead freight.

Sunday June 29. A fine calm morning but the sun is fearfully hot.
The usual service was held at 10 a.m. on the poop with an awning
overhead. Our little church looked very pretty with the seats placed
in a circle and covered with the flags of many nations. Our respected
clergyman preached one of his appropriate discourses, taking for his
text St Luke XIV 22 and inspired us with a feeling of deep respect.

We are all on deck together,
    On this fair Sabbath day;
In glowing tropic weather,
    Assembled here to pray;
While our stately ship continues
    Aghosting on her way.

4 p.m. The heat is suffocating and there is not enough wind to blow a fly off the sails. We are becalmed with every stitch of canvas sent aloft, and the ship appears like a drunken man, rolling back and forward without the slightest progress; however, the captain has been watching the distant horizon over our weather bow, and has ordered the Chief Officer to send all hands aloft to take in sail and make everything fast. Before the order was completed the bell rang for evening service. Our text tonight was Samuel book one, III, 14.

Before the sermon was finished darkness fell and with it came the storm. *Midnight.* The storm is still raging and the *Orient* is labouring hard. We are battened down below and almost stifled in the heat.

Then close they reef'd the timid sail,
    But every plank complaining loud,
We labour'd in the midnight gale,
    And ev'n our haughty mainmast bow'd.

Monday June 30. I passed a most miserable night lying most of it on the deck of my cabin in a state of nudity; the clothes in the bunk being saturated with perspiration. *5 a.m.* The storm is still raging. *9 a.m.* The weather has cleared and it looks like being a fine day. *11 a.m.* I was sitting in the stern bulwarks when I saw my first dolphin about a hundred yards from us. At 4 p.m. a shark was hovering about the ship on the lookout for a dainty morsel which was provided by a piece of salt pork covering a few inches of steel. This he found difficult to digest; but he was so voracious that at the same time he seized the bait and small hook belonging to a gentleman who was quietly bobbing for more harmless game from his cabin window. The shark was hauled on board and proved to be a young one, some eight feet long. After causing some merriment by his antics, he was dispatched and by order of the boatswain thrown overboard much to the annoyance of the ladies who wanted 'just another look at the dear creature'. *8 p.m.* Breeze freshening and a heavy squall is brewing on the lee bow. *Midnight.* It is very squally and intensely hot, pitch black and raining hard. We are running 9 knots.

The Ball on Shipboard, *by James Tissot* (*Tate Gallery, London*).

JULY

Tuesday July 1. 6 a.m. A fine morning and a fair wind. There is a sail in sight on our port bow, the first we have seen for eight days. *11 a.m.* A breeze sprang up from the SW and we are running 10 knots. *4 p.m.* The wind has dropped and it is scorching hot and calm. At the moment I am lazing in the captain's gig, the first time I have been outside the *Orient* for twenty-nine days. *10 p.m.* It is a beautiful night and we had a quadrille party on the poop and thoroughly enjoyed ourselves.

Wednesday July 2. Taken ill in the night and when I recovered I found myself on the saloon table and Doctor attending me; I was carried to my bunk and after a draft fell asleep. The Doctor informs me that the heat is turning me up; however, I feel considerably better this morning though not able to take my usual bath, or eat my breakfast.

I am not well and was lazing on a mattress on the poop this afternoon when one of the crew aloft dropped his marlinspike onto the poop not far from me; had it fallen on me I must have been pinned to the deck. The first mate yelled to him: 'Come down out of that you lazy lubber' and just as he was landing on deck the officer introduced a rope end to the tight part of his unmentionables, making him skidaddle to the forecastle quicker than he had intended.

10 p.m. We have been sailing up and down the Line for four days, the wind and sea being against us, and if we keep on this tack we shall run onto the coast of America. We want the SE Trades to take us across; by this time we ought to have been 30° S of the Line. All day we have been surrounded by large shoals of flying and other fish.

Thursday July 3. A fine morning and turned out at 6 a.m. I am considerably better though the doctor would not allow me to take a bath. Every morning all the gentlemen and nearly all the ladies enjoy its invigorating and healthy use, and in this heat it is looked forward to by everyone; but Jack Tar thinks differently. A notice was posted over the bath this morning:

> *Notice is hereby given that all persons, after this date, requiring more than three buckets of water for a bath in the morning, will be liable to a penalty not exceeding one bottle of grog weekly.*
>
> *By order of Swab.*

We are still on the wrong tack. Yesterday we were WSW and only gained 10 miles on the right course; today we are running ESE and have not gained a mile in the right direction. *Midday.* About ship again, now going WSW. It is fearfully hot. I hope this won't last much longer, it is awfully monotonous. The days are getting shorter, and will continue to do so as we go south. *10 p.m.* It is a fine calm night and the moon is just rising.

> Silent moon, if like Crotana's sage,
> By any spell my hand could dare
> To make thy disc its ample page
> And write my thoughts, my wish is there.
> How many a friend, whose careless eye
> Now wanders o'er that starry sky,
> Should smile upon thy orb to meet
> The recollections, kind and sweet;
> And all my heart and soul would send
> To many a dear loved, distant friend.
> How little when we parted last
> I thought those pleasant times were past;
> Little I knew that all were fled,
> That ere that summer's blooms were shed,
> My eye should see the sail unfurl'd
> That wafts me to the southern world;
> On such a blessed night as this
> I muse and think if friends were near,
> How we should feel, and gaze with bliss
> Upon the moon bright wavelets here.
> The sea is like a silvery lake,
> And o'er its calm the vessel glides
> Gently, as if it feared to wake
> The slumber of the silent tides;

> But hark! the boatswain's pipings tell
> 'Tis time to bid my dreams farewell;
> Eight bells, the middle watch is set,
> Goodnight beloved friends, ne'er forget
> That far beyond the Southern Sea
> Is one whose heart remembers thee!

Friday July 4. Feel unwell this morning. A stiff breeze blowing; we are running SW at 10 knots. At 8 a.m. a sail was seen on our weather bow; we ran up to her and signalled. She was a British transport with troops on board, homeward bound. *Noon.* A fine breeze and we are on our proper course bowling along at a slapping pace; we expect to cross the Line today. *4 p.m.* At last the Line is passed and the SE Trades are carrying our ship on her course. The captain's temper was wonderfully improved when on taking the sun at noon he found we were four miles south of the Line. I hope the worst is over and we shall experience fair winds and plenty of them.

A rumour has reached us from the forecastle that Old Neptune and his motley crew will board us tonight; the ladies and all the land-lubbers, myself included, are quaking with fear already, but as I am on the sick list I'll get doctor to ask Old Nep to give me a free pass; I don't feel equal to the 'brush and tar business'.

At 8 p.m. I was sitting on the poop watching the stars and thinking of home, when I was aroused by a stentorian voice shouting through a speaking trumpet 'Ship Ahoy, Ship Ahoy!' Immediately the whole forepart of the vessel was illuminated as if on fire; the ladies began to shriek, thinking they were about to be roasted or drowned; the captain sang out: 'Don't be alarmed ladies, it's only Father Neptune and his Wife come on Board'.

Sounds of merriment from the forecastle proclaimed that His Briny Majesty had arrived. Presently a mob of seamen approached the maindeck, fitted out in all the 'tag, rag and bobtail' that Jack so delights in; drawing a gun carriage on which sat Neptune, his Wife and Young Nep. Each seaman carried a lighted torch making the rabble appear like a set of demons. Old Neptune was almost naked, his skin smeared over with red chalk; his beard was unusually large, and on his head was a crown of tin. In his right hand he held a long trident upon which was stuck a young shark; his left arm was cuddled around Mother Neptune's neck, who appeared to be of the same colour and costume as her husband. Little Nep was the image of his father with the exception of the beard. On arriving at the quarter deck they halted and the captain was summoned to appear before Old Neptune. When they met the following conversation took place.

Neptune 'Well, my son, I welcome you to my dominions and con-

Crossing the line on board the Torrens. *One of those shown is said to be Joseph Conrad* (*Sunderland Art Gallery*).

gratulate you upon your safe arrival. Have you any landlubbers on board?'

Captain 'We have a few, but have you any letters for me?'

Neptune 'I have a packet of letters and a fish for your supper.'

Captain Won't you come on the poop and see the ladies?'

Neptune 'Thank you, I can't stay any longer, I have three other ships to board tonight.'

Captain 'What have you been doing to your wife; I see she has a black eye.' (There was a black rag stuck on the left cheek.)

Neptune 'Oh, the old basket and I had a damned row last night, but we're all square again now, ain't we old gal?' and a process of kissing and hugging was gone through to the delight of the ladies on the poop.

Captain 'Well, if you won't stay we'd better say goodnight. We want to get on our way.'

After this three unfortunate middies had to undergo the operation of shaving. Neptune and his gang then retired to the forecastle and soon a large tar tub in flames was floating in our wake. This was Neptune in his chariot of fire taking his departure to his briny home. The letter which he had left behind was then read out:

Equator July 4th, 1862

Dear Friends,

I have now come to receive you with a hearty welcome to the Southern Climes. It is always with great pleasure that I board an English merchantman, having tested in days of yore the generosity of all British subjects.

I boarded a vessel a few days ago from London and with great pleasure I was informed that my favourite ship, *Orient,* was shortly expected, for I have a great partiality for regular traders that come this way. I must now conclude with my hearty thanks to you for the generosity you have shown to my sons by drinking my health at your expense.

Wishing you all a more favourable passage than you have hitherto had, and a hearty welcome to the land of gold.

I remain

Your fishy friend

Neptune

'Adieu'

Midnight. It is blowing hard and the sea is getting rough; I'll turn in as I'm feeling tired and not very well.

Saturday July 5. 7 a.m The sea is rough and the wind high; we are running 10 knots close hauled. *11 a.m.* There is a heavy gale. I was on the poop watching the huge waves rolling by when a squall struck us. The ship lurched and away I went into the lee scuppers like an apple, at the same time I heard an awful crash overhead. I got on my legs, looked up, and saw the mainroyal and maintopgallant were carried away and the mainmast was a wreck of ropes and spars; immediately all passengers were ordered below and both watches sent aloft to clear away the wreckage. *4 p.m.* The roughest day we have had for some time, blowing hard and continually shipping seas. *11 p.m.* It is a very stormy night and the crew, poor fellows, are all up aloft rigging a temporary maintopgallant and royal. The captain expects to lose his fore and aft royals before morning. *Midnight.* A few minutes ago I was sitting on the edge of my bunk when the *Orient,* as if for devilment, gave a lurch and sent me headfirst onto the wash-stand causing a general smash amongst the crockery, and affording much fun to my shipmate who was curled up in his bunk, screaming with laughter. Although it was a nasty experience, I had to join in with him; I don't think there will be much sleep for us tonight.

Sunday July 6. 8 a.m. No sleep last night, the hatchway was battened down and we nearly smothered. *Noon.* Church service was held in the saloon owing to the rough weather. *10 p.m.* A fine moonlit night and the wind and sea have gone down. We are off the coast of South America running at 10 knots.

Monday July 7. A fine morning and I turned out at 6 a.m.; feel much better in health. The ship is going along steadily; all hands aloft rigging up a new main topgallant mast in place of the one we lost on Saturday. *Noon.* Dirty weather set in again; squalls, headwinds, and high seas; we are running close hauled out of our course. *10 p.m.* Another fearfully rough night and squalls constantly overtaking us;

the skipper has just given the word to pipe all hands on deck to 'about ship'. We are running too close to the coast of America, being only one degree off the Brazils.* Poor *Orient,* you seem fated to be tied to bad winds, squalls and calms. On Saturday morning it seemed as though all the 'dirt' in the vicinity was collecting to give us a benefit. Squalls followed squalls from early dawn to . . . 'here comes another'. I'll drop the pen and get into my bunk.

Tuesday July 8. 7 a.m. The wind died away before daylight and the sea is now much calmer. *10 p.m.* It has been a beautiful day; one of the finest we have had; we are still off the coast of America; the skipper has ordered the sounding lead to be ready and the main anchor to be dropped over the bows in case we should be driven too close in during the night. *Midnight.* Squally, dirty night and a turbulent sea running.

Wednesday July 9. A dirty morning with squally weather and a head wind that is making the ship roll back and forward in a most uncomfortable manner. *Noon.* The weather is a little more settled. Captain Harris has kindly furnished me with the history of our superb ship for my log.

The *Orient* was built in 1853 by Messrs Thomas Bilbe, Perry and Co. in Nelson Dock, London, and is 1,030 tons burden. She is a favourite ship and much sought after by passengers, especially colonists, and on one of her homeward trips carried 94 passengers of all classes. If we arrive safely this passage she will have made six voyages to Adelaide, her sole port of destination except in 1853† when

---

*Until the second half of the nineteenth century ships sailing to Australia traversed the eastern shores of the South Atlantic, passing near to the Cape of Good Hope; the Western Atlantic with its lee shore was avoided ; Cape San Rocque having a particularly unsavoury reputation. Using the old route, 120 days was considered fast. An American oceanographer, Matthew Fontaine Maury (1806–73) was the first to advocate the western route for the fast weatherly ships of the 1850s, sailing on a Great Circle from Cape San Rocque southwards to reach the high latitudes, up to 55° s, as quickly as possible, making maximum use of the se Trades. Maury's advice shortened the journey by some forty days. A very important qualification of the Great Circle route was that only powerful, well-founded vessels could venture far into the fifties without unwise strain on equipment and personnel.

Captain Harris followed Maury's suggested course, though his furthest south was 45° 43′ s, 115° 30′ e.

†The *Orient* was built to carry passengers in the gold boom at Melbourne, and had a poop 61 feet long for this purpose, but for her maiden journey she was used as a troop carrier to the Crimea. At the landing at Alma in September 1854 she was transport No. 78 carrying the Connaught Rangers. She survived the gale off Balaclava, on November 14th, 1854, when 34 Allied ships were lost and over 1,000 men. In October 1855 she was used as a hospital ship in the expedition against Kinburn and Odessa. In 1856 she returned to London, and began sailing on the Adelaide run with a full passenger list and a high reputation.

she was first built and was chartered by the British Government, and sent to the Crimea as a hospital ship for the wounded during the war with Russia. Except during her homeward trip from the Crimea, when Captain Balentine commanded her, and for this voyage when we sail under Captain Harris, Captain Lawrence has always had the command, and by his urbanity and general courtesy rendered himself a favourite with all who sailed with him; and under him she made one of the quickest passages on record to Adelaide, viz. in 75 days.*

Her total length is 215 feet, her breadth 36 feet, her mainmast rises, 145 feet from the decks, and 24 feet below. When in full sail she carries 43 sails and upwards of 4,800 square yards of canvas, and uses upwards of 1,900 fathoms of rope of all sorts to rig and fix the same.

Besides our captain, there are four mates. Mr Train, the first, has made many voyages in her; and bound to the ship are eight apprentices or midshipmen, England's future sea captains. The crew consist of eighteen able and two ordinary seamen under the immediate command of the boatswain; a head steward and four under; with three cooks, two stock keepers, one butcher, and two watermen to look after the eating department; three carpenters, and two sail makers. Including passengers there are 108 in all, who require large quantities of provisions, both fresh and salt. We left Plymouth with 28 sheep, 18 pigs and a sow in pig, 20 dozen fowl, 10 dozen ducks, 4 dozen geese, 8 dozen turkeys, a cow and a calf, the latter has been turned into veal. Immense supplies of preserved and salt provisions lie in the 'tween decks, sufficient for the outward and homeward voyage, the exact quantity being known only to that wandering soul, the steward; but over a thousand eggs will be consumed on the voyage.

There is a miscellaneous cargo of freight, and the following livestock: 36 rams, 3 dogs, 20 rabbits, 2 horses, and a whole host of birds, goldfish and other pets for our colonial friends.

Thursday July 10. I witnessed a splendid sunrise at 7 a.m. It is a fine morning, but a dead calm. There is a ship in sight over the stern, in the same predicament as ourselves, becalmed. *11 a.m.* A breeze sprang up and sent us flying along; the ship in our wake tried hard to catch us so the captain took in sail and waited for her to see if she wanted anything. She proved to be the *Tyburnia*† from London to Bombay, sailing six days before us; she signalled for a supply of flour,

---

*This compares favourably with some of the *Cutty Sark's* best runs from Australia carrying wool. Between 1883 and 1895 from Sydney N.S.W. or Newcastle N.S.W. she averaged about 75 days. In 1885 Sydney to the Downs 73 days. 1889–90 Sydney–London 75 days. 1887 Newcastle–Lizard 69 days. 1891–2 Sydney–Lizard 83 days.

†Extract from *Lloyd's Registry of Shipping,* 1862: the ship *Tyburnia* of 1,027 tons, captain F. Coote, was built in Glasgow in 1857 for Somes Bros. She was registered in London and traded with India.

but as we were on short allowance we could not spare any. The two captains signalled to each other for more than an hour, and arranged to keep company during the night and burn blue lights occasionally as we were close on the South American coast off St Salvador. Yesterday we were off Rio San Francisco. The *Tyburnia* reports herself 43 days out, all well.

Midnight.   I have just been on deck looking at the two ships signalling to each other with blue lights; our consort lay off about a mile and a half, and when exhibiting the light looked very pretty, and no doubt we looked the same to them when showing ours; they will continue burning lights until day-break as we are near the Hotspur Shoals.

Friday July 11. 6 a.m.   A fine morning and the *Tyburnia* is sailing along comfortably on our lee quarter about three miles off. *10 a.m.* Another ship in sight ahead of us; clapped on sail and made up to her and discovered her to be the *Blanche Moore** from Liverpool to Melbourne with 400 emigrants on board. After the usual signalling a boat commanded by the first mate made for the ship that lay two miles away. After an hour and a half they returned with a small stock of flour, which, despite the supply from the Dutchman, was still wanted on board. The boat returned with sundry presents for our emigrating friends, in the shape of potatoes, novels and newspapers. Soon after their departure a boat was lowered from the *Blanche Moore* containing about a dozen passengers and officers who were welcomed on board the *Orient,* and after a slight report, made a tour of the ship, but were soon obliged to return to their own vessel, amid adieux from the passengers who vied with each other to cheer the loudest; shortly afterwards our boat returned, well pleased with their visit and the courteous behaviour of the captain of the *Blanche Moore.* Our visitors left behind the following small memento:

The Chief Officer, Purser, and saloon passengers of the Blanche Moore *beg to return their thanks to the captain and saloon passengers of the* Orient *for the very kind reception given them on board, and hope they will have a quick and prosperous voyage.*

> When o'er the empty seas alone,
> For days and nights in silence roam;
> They who've felt it know how sweet,
> Some sunny morn a sail to meet.
>
> Sparkling at once is every eye,
> 'Ship ahoy, ship ahoy' our joyful cry!
> While answering back the sounds we hear,
> 'Ship ahoy, ship ahoy, What cheer, what cheer?'

*The *Blanche Moore* is not recorded in *Lloyd's Registry of Shipping.*

> Then sails are backed, we nearer come,
> Kind words are said of friends and home;
> And soon, too soon, we part with pain,
> To sail o'er silent sea again.

Midnight. A fine moonlight night with a calm sea and very hot. The *Tyburnia* is on our lee quarter, about two miles off, again burning blue lights; the *Blanche Moore* was far astern at sundown and we have seen the last of her.

Saturday July 12. The *Tyburnia* is still on our lee quarter, and straining every stitch of canvas to keep up with us. *10 p.m.* It has been a splendid day with a light breeze and running on our course SSE all day.

Sunday July 13. 8 a.m. A fine breeze and running at 10 knots. The *Tyburnia* is on the weather side but cannot get ahead of us do what she will. She is a splendid sailor and our skipper has just sent up the British Ensign to give her our usual morning salute. *10 a.m.* The bell is ringing for church, and the ladies are all dressed in summer attire and look charming.

10 p.m. A most beautiful day and we have made a good run at 10 knots throughout; our consort is now a long way astern and cannot keep up with Miss Orient. Captain Harris has just ordered the spanker and topgallantsail to be brought down to allow our friend to come up and keep us company during the night.

At 6 o'clock everyone was on deck to witness a tropical sunset at sea. I cannot convey an adequate representation of the scene, or describe my feelings and those of my fellow passengers as we stared in breathless silence at the sun dipping beneath the horizon; scarcely had we recovered from a trance of enchantment when our attention was drawn to the east and the full moon floated on the water like an immense ball of fire until it rose into the sky.

Midnight. The *Tyburnia* has caught up and is on our weather side about four miles off. We will remain together until morning; then if we get a fair wind the captain has decided to clap on all sail and bid our friend goodbye.

Monday July 14. I was so delighted with the sunset last night that I turned out at daybreak to see it rise. First the moon, looking very sombrous as if weary of its night's work, sank into the sea over our lee bow. Presently Old Sol appeared in a magnificent display, and the inhabitants of the deep came to the surface to greet him. We could see a whale sporting on the surface and blowing up a huge fountain of water, while his shrill whistle was clearly heard. Not far from him scores of porpoises were rolling one after the other like a lot of skipjacks, followed by shoals of flying fish; even the pretty dolphin showed himself.

6 p.m.   We have had a fine breeze all day and are running 12 knots; the *Tyburnia* is in sight but almost hull down and we don't expect to see her in the morning. She has maintained a class race with us, from the first time we saw her last Thursday till this evening when she stood away to the east and will soon be lost to view. At times she was a little ahead of us and though it caused excitement on board, we knew that give the *Orient* wind and her head, and there are few ships afloat that will leave her astern. We kept up a running fire of signals with the *Tyburnia* and her captain seemed to know we were beating him, for in one of his last he paid us the compliment of saying, 'You are a fast sailor.' The reply was, 'Stale news, captain', and he found his compliment was no empty one.

Midnight.   Everyone seems inclined to remain on deck, it is such a lovely night, calm, hot and no wind. We enjoyed another beautiful sunset this evening; I was on the forecastle smoking my pipe and watching the groups of seamen clustered together, spinning yarns and singing songs; some were listening to the hilarity going on in the saloon cabin, for the heat had rendered it necessary to open the skylights; others were paying equal attention to the vocal talents of honest Jack, who made up his deficiency in the grace and talent of his superiors, by his peculiar and characteristic humour. The moon

The Ship, *by William Holman Hunt (Tate Gallery, London).*

shone with crystalline clearness and the gentle motion of the ship threw the shadows of the rigging in corresponding movement on the deck; I was thinking of England when I heard the following conversation:

'I say, Bill' shouted one of the lookouts on the forecastle, addressing his mate as he looked to windward; 'I don't much like the looks of the sky thereaway; to my thinking it's somewhat fiery eyed.' Without moving from his position the other man replied: 'I'd ha' thought you would have known better Jim, it's only the pride of the sun, to show his glory to the last; would you have him go out like a purser's dip, a spark and away?' 'Well, we live and learn as long as there's a flurry of breath in the windsel,' and he gave the mountain of tobacco in his cheek a twist; 'I like to see a good sunset, and I never see'd finer than in these here seas; it seems strange to me that God Almighty should have made this part of the world so beautiful and so empty.' At this point the mate of the watch shouted from the quarter deck: 'Keep a good lookout forrard there!' 'Aye, Aye, sir,' replied Jim, and then added in a low tone: 'They're having a jolly time in the cabin.' 'It's a sad heart as never rejoices' said the boatswain who had just joined them, 'but I don't like the look o' that sky to windward, it's a parting blush o' sun, or a gathering squall o' the night.'

I left the poop and sat with the doctor for an hour and then went below and turned in. During the middle watch as I lay in my bunk, not having been asleep I heard the first mate bellow: 'Hard up with the helm, hard a weather!' I slipped on my clothes and went on deck; the sea was a sheet of foam, the wind came whistling like ten thousand arrows; a report like the discharge of a heavy piece of artillery came from forr'd, and the jib flew away in a fleecy cloud to leeward; the vessel heeled over carrying everybody and everything into the lee scuppers; the lightning hissed and cracked as it exploded between the masts, making everything tremble from keel to the trucks; broad sheets of water were lifted up and dashed over the decks fore and aft, as the gale tried to plunge the vessel beneath the waves. As she struggled to lift herself against the tempest the topsail halliards were let go, but the nearly horizontal position of the mast prevented the sails from running down, and destruction threatened, when crack, away went the topmast over the side, the spanker sheet was cut away and the spanker followed the jib. The ship partially righted herself, and Captain Harris and the officers rushed on deck, but the squall had passed; the moon shone again and the deceitful ocean was all smiles as if nothing had happened; though the evidence was all too plain in the dismantled state of our ship. All hands were called on deck to clear away the wreck, and the passengers were sent below out of the way of falling spars.

Tuesday July 15. 7 a.m. A fine morning and a splendid breeze; all hands are aloft repairing last night's damage. The skipper is scanning the horizon to see if the *Tyburnia* is in sight, and to know how she behaved in the squall, but we are alone and there is nothing to be seen.
Wednesday July 16. All last night we ran 15 knots. We are getting clear of the tropics and it is not so hot this morning. There is a splendid breeze and we are running 14 knots. *10 p.m.* A dark night, the sea is rough and rather cold.
Thursday July 17. Cold, wet weather has set in. During the middle watch a squall passed over and took away the favourable wind. *10 a.m.* We are surrounded by numerous cape pigeons and albatrosses. There is no wind, the sea is rough and the ship is tumbling about like a log. *4 p.m.* A miserable day and little progress, though we ought not to grumble as the last few days we have had splendid wind. No vessel we have come across has taken the lead from the *Orient.* Long may she continue thus.

It is gradually getting colder, and each day warmer costumes appear; at present it is delightful and most agreeable after the great heat of the tropics.
Friday July 18. It is dark now at 6 a.m. Turned out at 7 a.m. but it was dull and cold with no sun. *10 p.m.* Cold and misty all day with a very heavy swell. We are in the latitude of the Cape of Good Hope, but 1400 miles west of it.
Saturday July 19. 10 p.m. It has been a very rough day with a strong wind and the sea running high. We had to take in sails and are now running under double reefed topsails, and shipping seas every ten minutes; few ladies appeared on deck the last day or two as it is too cold for them. Last week they were only too glad to remain on deck night and day, the weather was so hot.
Sunday July 20. A very stormy night and shipping seas all the while; our cabins are drenched. Both watches were called on deck to work the pumps. I had no sleep and was pitched out of my bunk twice. *4 p.m.* A heavy gale; no passengers are permitted on deck today, they would soon be washed off. The ship is lying over on her lee bulwarks. *10 p.m.* The gale is freshening, and driving us along at 15 knots with scarcely any canvas up.
Monday July 21. Another very rough night and few of us went to bed; if we did we were pitched out by the lurching of the ship. During the middle watch the two starboard guns on the quarter deck broke loose and crushed the left arm of one of the forecastle men; the poor fellow is now a cripple. The sea is mountains high and on the weather side the bulwarks are gone fore and aft; no passengers are allowed on deck and the hatchways are battened down to keep out the water. *10 p.m.* The gale has continued all day and the men are still at work at the pumps. *Midnight.* The gale is moderating and the sea going

down. We are all beginning to feel very miserable having been confined below so long and smacked about like so many rats in a tub. I'll try my bunk again and hope for a good night's rest.

Tuesday July 22. Woke at 8 a.m. after a refreshing sleep. The wind and sea are quieter this morning. *10 p.m.* The weather is more settled; all hands have been at work repairing damage done by the gale, the figurehead was found to have lost an arm, either blown or washed away. I hope the old gal has not received any serious injury; perhaps it is the loss of the arm that makes the ship give such lurches!

Wednesday July 23. It is nearly dark at 8 a.m. now, so rose at 8.30. Squally weather with hail showers and high seas causing the ship to lurch, to the horror of the steward and danger to the crockery, which is sent flying in every direction; while the contents of sundry soup tureens, etc., hardly improve the dress of any unlucky lady who may happen to be in the way, but at the same time causing amusement to all, for the greater the lurch the greater the laughter.

Thursday July 24. I am getting tired of this squally, gloomy and dirty weather as we are confined so much below, but to make up the wind is blowing us on the right course at a spanking rate. Today we have run 320 miles.*

Friday July 25. Thick, rainy weather with squalls all day. I have been unwell again, the confinement below does not agree with me.

Saturday July 26. Very ill today and could not eat. Overcast and raining. At noon one of the forecastle men caught a fine specimen of a mollyhawk and brought it below for the passengers to see. It was a large bird and had been driven on board to seek shelter from the storm. It was seven feet seven inches from wing to wing, and forty-two inches from bill to tail.

Sunday July 27. The ship is labouring very heavily through confused seas, and I feel very sick this morning. Only the morning service was held today, and that under great difficulties. *10 p.m.* A sudden squall has just torn our mizen topsail into ribbons.

Monday July 28. The ship is pitching very heavily, and the sky is dark and squally. I feel better today, having been on deck for an hour or two.

Our quiet community was startled today by a dextrous robbery of a ham, which was stolen from the safe on the poop. I think the safe has belied its name in allowing the ham to escape so easily; it is said a savoury smell was observable in the vicinity of the 'Middies' quarters last night.†

*This was a fine achievement. The famous tea clipper *Thermopylae's* best day's run was probably 348 miles running her easting down in 1875 under Captain Matheson. It is also said that *Sobraon* under Captain Elmslie RNR did 340 miles in 24 hours.

†One of these midshipmen became the well-known sailing master Captain Thomas Yardley Powles.

Tuesday July 29. 10 p.m. Very squally, and lightning in the south-east. Today for amusement it was proposed to hold a lottery of the ship's passage; and a subscription list was filled under the following regulations:

To consist of 32 tickets, each ticket to be marked with a date, commencing with August 1st, and ending with September 1st (Nautical time) and drawn from a hat one at a time; tickets to be 2/6 each, and the drawer of the date either of the pilot coming on board, or anchoring at the Lightship, Adelaide (whichever happened first) to have the prize of £4; but if the ship arrived after September 1st, the money to be returned; disputes, if any, to be referred to the captain.

Wednesday July 30. 10 p.m. Ugly, dirty sky and lightning all over the horizon. The glass is falling and two whirlwinds passed us about noon travelling ENE carrying away our fore topsails and royals. No passengers allowed on deck today; all battened down below. Rounding the Cape* is rough work!

Thursday July 31. 8 p.m. We have been through a hurricane with squalls, rain and lightning all day. The ship behaves nobly, the only canvas we have aloft is the fore topsail to keep her head down. We lost the captain's gig; a mountain wave came rolling on top of us and washed it away; the last few days and nights, to say the least, have been very uncomfortable. Continual storms, rain and bad weather necessitate staying below, causing headaches and drowsiness followed by *ennui* and thin attendance at breakfast; many preferring that meal in their cabins, and endeavouring afterwards to seek a little sleep denied them during the night by the terrible rolling of the ship; however, we are progressing on our way, and amid the trials that attend us, this cheers all; even our good captain, whose face is both compass and barometer.

AUGUST

Friday August 1. A repetition of yesterday; thunder, lightning, rain, variable winds, heavy confused sea and the ship labouring hard at intervals. There was no sleep last night, everything was tumbling topsyturvy. The doctor's medicine chest broke from its moorings and turned sundry bottles upside down, causing chaos among the salts which strewed the floor.

Last night was the worst storm we have had yet; all yesterday squalls were frequent, but as night came on it began to blow in good earnest; at times one would fancy sufficient to drive us bodily into the sea; lightning accompanied with terrific peals of thunder illuminated

*The Cape of Good Hope.

the whole sky, adding if possible to the effect of the sea, whose waves were running mainyard high; while a storm of hail and rain made matters worse for those obliged to remain on deck The two men at the helm were lashed to the wheel to prevent them from being washed overboard.

This afternoon I watched the course of a whirlwind; happily we escaped its vortex, but felt its effects very severely in the gale which followed. A white squall would have been equally interesting had not its violence rendered a retreat below absolutely necessary.

Saturday August 2. Another rough night; the gale seems determined to try our ship, her spars and yards; happily all prove sound, and no accident of any consequence occurred, despite the wind blowing at times with great fury from ssw to NW, and a tremendous confused sea which knocked the ship about, and shook everyone out of their bunks; however, it has gone down somewhat, though still enough to make writing difficult.

Sunday August 3. Had a tolerably good night's rest; the gale moderated and the sea was calmer by morning; it is cold now and the middle watch reported that during the night we passed close to what was thought to be a ship, but it was too dark to be sure; the captain thinks it was an iceberg. This shows the necessity of a vigilant lookout, particularly in these latitudes where icebergs abound. They are ugly customers especially in fog, such as has attended us this week. *10 p.m.* Today we passed over with the usual accompaniment of praise to our good God, who has hitherto carried us across the mighty deep and preserved us from its dangers.

Monday August 4. Turned out at 8 a.m. A misty cold morning, but fine. The last few days we have been accompanied by large numbers of those pretty birds, the cape pigeons who seem sent by Providence to cheer the hearts of mariners on their dreary voyages. *10 p.m.* We have made a good run today. For some time the sea-going qualities of our ship have been tested in no ordinary degree. We have been tossed about by wind and tempestuous seas, and when seated at the breakfast table the faces around tell tales of sleepless nights and sickness; but the ship has passed the ordeal unscathed, and we cannot speak too highly of the energy and assiduity of those who have brought us in safety across the trackless sea.

Tuesday August 5. Overcast and misty with a fair wind and extremely cold. This morning a large iceberg passed on our weather side about three miles off. *10 p.m.* A birth on board! Great excitement this morning especially among the ladies, when it was announced that the shepherd bitch had brought six pups into the world, 'all alive and kicking'. No dog, not even Punch's Toby, received so much attention or excited so much interest as did the mother of six pups born in a bird cage. They are being nursed and caressed by the ladies, who are always requesting to have just another look, particularly at the bobtailed one.

Wednesday August 6.   Squally, rain and fog; hitherto grumbling seems to have been my principal theme, though now and then a word of hope for the future creeps in; but ill luck continually attends our good ship; rain, continual rain seems our portion, but what need we mind when the wind continues favourably and plenty of it?

Thursday August 7.   Very dirty weather today, squally, fog and rain. Our amusements have lately been at a discount; the ladies seem to have a growing liking for the quiet of their cabins; this may be the fault of the gentlemen who have been remiss in their gallantry, or perhaps, and most likely, the rain which has fallen almost continually for a week has caused drowsiness. The piano, too, has been out of tune which added to our discomfort.

Friday August 8.   Having been awake most of the night I did not turn out until dinner time. The weather is miserably cold and dirty, squally, thick fog and rain. A suicide was committed this morning. A Mr Blackbird, with a rashness before unheard of, jumped overboard, the door of his cage having been accidently left open. Our feathered songsters enliven our dull and monotonous existence; on shutting your eyes you might fancy, minus the rocking of the ship, that you were ashore; in many of the cabins a canary or two is to be found; two in the cuddy seem to vie with each other to sing the loudest, and during meals keep up a continual duet. Now and then a blackbird, thrush or lark, a little more lively than his brothers, sends forth a note; but I am sorry to say many of the birds have died from one cause or another, and their number is now hardly a tithe of that when we left Plymouth. I hope those left will reach Adelaide and enliven the hearts of many exiled from their native land.

At times the cow proclaims her presence with a soniferous note; the squeals of the pigs are rather too often heard, and a regular chorus is maintained by the ducks and chickens on the poop, particularly when the butcher heaves in sight; now and then a ram, his thoughts perhaps reverting to the green hills of England, or impatient for dinner, informs the public of his ideas. *10 p.m.* A very dark night, cold and foggy.

Saturday August 9.   Squally, foggy and rain as usual.

> God speed the stately *Orient,*
>   And bear her safely o'er
> The foaming waves that roll towards
>   Australia's distant shore.
>
> In those dear isles we love so well,
>   But now so far away,

Are loving friends and kindred dear
   Who for our safety pray.

Many a heart would swell with grief,
   And tears dim many eyes,
If aught befell the gallant bark
   As o'er the deep she flies.

A noble crew directs her course,
   Stout hearts and steady hands;
But all in vain without His aid
   Who winds and waves commands.

Swift as the birds that round her fly,
   She cleaves her watery way;
Graceful she parts the heaving tides
   'Mid clouds of foam and spray.

And as He guides the seabird's flight
   Safe through the tempest's roar;
May He guide the *Orient's* path
   Swift to the southern shore.

Sunday August 10. 10 p.m. The weather was rough, misty, hard winds and very dirty. Divine Service was held in the saloon cabin, but the rolling of the ship made it difficult to stand.

Monday August 11. Arose at 8 a.m. Heavy squalls with hail. *10 p.m.* There is a gale blowing, and the patent of the main topsail yard has broken. The passengers are all battened below.

Tuesday August 12. I passed a sleepless night, but the weather has moderated this morning.

Wednesday August 13. 8 p.m. One of the fine rams belonging to the Hon. J. Baker died today; no fault is due to anyone on board, the greatest care having been taken of these valuable animals. This one had been sickly from the start of the voyage. Shortly after its death it was opened and showed a mass of disease; it must have suffered excruciating pain for some time, and death was the greatest mercy.

Thursday August 14. Another miserable day, drizzling rain and very dark in the north-east.

Friday August 15. Squalls and rain.

Saturday August 16. On going on deck this morning found everything damp, dirty and unpleasant. *10 p.m.* I spent the day in my bunk as the warmest place I could find, reading a book lent to me by the doctor; this evening a festive scene took place in the saloon, the birthday of a young lady on board being marked by some champagne presented by the unmarried gentlemen. I wish more of these interesting events had happened during the voyage as they produce much merriment.

Sunday August 17. As usual, squally, and the ship labouring heavily; as consolation we have a fair wind and are nearing land, and our long journey will soon be over. Next week we hope to be in Adelaide, and the weather is getting much warmer.

Monday August 18. 8 p.m. Shortly after noon we passed Cape Leeuwin, and now we are in Australian waters, and if the wind proves moderately favourable this will be quite an average passage in spite of our previous forebodings. From Plymouth to Cape Leeuwin in 73 days, and from the Cape of Good Hope to Cape Leeuwin in 11 days is cause for congratulation to all, especially to our good captain for whose sake, if for no other reason, we have wished a short and pleasant passage.

Tuesday August 19. Turned out at 7 a.m. Raining and variable winds. Everyone is calculating the number of days before we arrive at our destination, and we think this will be our last week on board, a joyous thought tinged with sorrow at parting with many kind friends, albeit of only a few months – acquaintances, perhaps. We shall soon be scattered according to our respective vocations and may never meet again, yet those who have shared the dangers of the depths together will never be strangers to each other.

When we land on the shore of Australia we will meet new scenes and faces, but we shall still be subjects of our widowed Queen, sharing our loyalty to that sovereign over whose dominions 'the sun never sets'.

The following paragraph and verse was found posted on the door of the saloon cabin this morning:

The passage of the Orient *drawing to a close, 'Old Salt' the father of all sailors cannot part with his children (the ladies and gentlemen passengers of the* Orient) *without a sincere prayer for their health and happiness in the land of their adoption and so:*

> With every joy and pleasure gay,
>   May all their hours roll sweet along;
> Till life and beauty glide away,
>   Like the rich cadence of a song.
>
> May friendship shed its gentle rays,
>   Surround their path and make it bright;
> And love serenely gild their days,
>   With a more pure and holy light.

And in that future happy time,
    Their earlier friends, perchance forgot,
Say, will they read this careless rhyme,
    And the Old *Orient* remember not?

Remember not, and can it be
    The joyous memory ever die;
That all my heart doth feel for them
    Is but fleeting whispered sigh?

Yes, it is written in our lot,
    That lot so varied, dark, and strange,
We meet, we part, and are forgot,
    In painful and perpetual change.

But why this idle gloom on me,
    Oh be again the gay and free;
They will not to their dying day
    Forget the Old *Orient* or me.

> I remain, Ladies and Gentlemen,
> Yours sincerely,
> Old Salt (Father of all sailors).

Wednesday August 20.   Squally but not so cold; every eye is strained to get a glimpse of land and excitement prevails among passengers and crew; the captain having offered two sovereigns to the person who first sights land. I think one of the crew will obtain the prize; a man is perched like a bird at the masthead peering at the horizon to get a sight of mother earth. *10 p.m.* A hard gale and the glass in falling.

Thursday August 21. 8 a.m. We passed a rough night. This morning about 11 o'clock we heard 'Land Ahoy, Land Ahoy' from the masthead. Everyone immediately swarmed on deck, but for a time were disappointed, as land could only be seen by those at the mastheads; however, later in the day Kangaroo Island hove in sight. The wind is in the north and we shall have to beat up the gulf, and it may yet be two or three days before we drop anchor.

Friday August 22.   Turned out at 4.30 a.m. *10 p.m.* Contrary winds all day, about ship every four hours, a fine night. Before leaving the ship it has been decided to present the following testimonials to the captain and the doctor:

To Capt. J. Harris and the Chief Officer of the ship *Orient*.
    We the undersigned passengers per ship *Orient* beg to tender our sincere thanks to Capt. Harris and his chief officer Mr Irvine, for

their kind attention and universal desire to please during a very pleasant passage, and at the same time our congratulations on the speedy termination of what at first promised, through contrary winds and bad weather, to be a long voyage.

Ship *Orient* August 22nd, 1862.

(Signature of all the passengers follows.)

To Dr. F. G. Nash F.R.C.P.

Dear Sir,

We cannot allow you to depart from amongst us without expressing to you the feelings of deep regard that your presence during the voyage has inspired within us, and request to be permitted to bear testimony in this humble manner, to the uniform courtesy and friendship that you have invariably shown towards all, apart from any reference to that medical skill and kind attention you have exhibited in, fortunately, the few cases that have required your attention. We trust the voyage has proved a pleasant one to you, and that when we separate, though perhaps it should not be our lot to meet again, you will sometimes bestow a thought upon those who, wishing you every success and happiness, and a speedy return to your family, beg to inscribe themselves:

Your sincere friends

(Here follow signatures of all the passengers)

Ship *Orient* 22nd August 1862.

Saturday August 23.   Turned out at 6 a.m. to a fine morning, wind still against us. Kangaroo Island was not in view, and we expect to sight the mainland before sundown. Everyone is busy gathering up their goods and preparing for a general rush on shore as soon as we cast anchor.

> I am going to tell you without any flam,
> All about the passengers that am
> On board the *Orient* clipper.
> Well, shuffle the lot, and when you've dealed,
> Up came the Rev. Thos. and Mrs Field:
> Then next there comes, for they're all the go,
> From the Assembly Room, Cassing and Co.
> And after that comes Mr and Mrs Small,
> Both very young, somewhat short, so not tall:
> Then most obliging of ladies, Mrs Masters;
> And her who sings 'Caroline Plasters' –
> It is, of course, I mean Miss Nielson,
> Then Miss Hill, so full of frolic and fun,
> Then, of the gents, there's so meek and quiet,

Two views of the port of Adelaide in 1840 and 1888. Edward Lacey's arrival was midway between.

Curious, machine-making, Mr Wyatt;
And, the most useful Mr Marshall;
Then, Mr Varndell called Betsy, not Val;
And his charming cousin, Mr Faulkener,
Though it is said he don't talk much; nor
Long legged, but good hearted Mr Walker,
And whom they also say is no talker;
But as I near the end, up comes Carnie,
Always laughing, and so full of blarney;
And to wind up with, there's Mr Lacey,
A rummy cove, who except at dinner times, is jolly lazy.

10 p.m. The contrary winds prevented us reaching land before sundown; we have been tacking about-ship all day. *Midnight.* The masthead lookout has just spied the Cape Border light on our lee bow.
Sunday August 24. Arose at 6 a.m. A beautiful morning and we are now running up the Gulf of St Vincent. There is a splendid view of the land which is about six miles to leeward. *Midnight.* We are safely at anchor at the lightship about nine miles from Port Adelaide.

We had Divine Service twice today and passengers and crew assembled on the poop to offer up prayers to the Almighty for watching over us during our long and perilous voyage. I believe prayers were never more fervently offered than today; it was a most impressive sight and one I shall ever remember, to see our respected clergyman in his white surplice kneeling on the deck surrounded by his fellow passengers, all with bended knee and deeply impressed with the solemnity of the occasion.

146

I will now turn into my bunk for the last time. Tomorrow I leave the *Orient,* and stand for the first time on my future home, Australia. Now the moment has almost arrived to leave the good old ship I feel as if I were about to separate from a faithful friend: she has carried me safely over 16,000 miles of angry sea and sheltered me through many a raging storm. I hope she may be spared to carry me back to England again.

> Oh, may those she safely carried
>   From friends at home to these distant lands,
> Find health and peace; and all they hoped for
>   Attend the labour of their hands.

Monday August 25.   I turned out of my bunk for the last time at 6 a.m. Last night at sundown the pilot came on board, also the Customs House Officers, and the Ship's Agent. We are still (7 a.m.) at anchor waiting for the tide to take the ship up to the Port. The wind has been from the north and we have had to beat up the Gulf; with a favourable wind we should have made a splendid passage; as it is 82 days looks remarkably well, and must cause great pleasure to our good captain. *11 a.m.*   The captain has just informed me his gig is now being got ready to take him on shore, and he has kindly offered to take me with him, and as I am under orders to report myself to the Chief Secretary immediately upon my arrival in the colony, I will avail myself of the captain's offer; so I must bid a hasty farewell to my fellow passengers, pack up my traps, and prepare to land in this new country where I have to commence life afresh and where all are entire strangers. Let me say goodbye to the good ship *Orient,* her officers and crew.

Edwd. Lacey
Ship *Orient,* Port Adelaide, S.A. August 25th, 1862.

APPENDIX A
Sails and Rigging

The plans reproduced on the following pages illustrate the rigging and sails of the three-masted ship and barque. The barque had several advantages over the ship; the chief of these being economy. She required fewer hands, fewer spars, less canvas and less cordage; while the difference in speed, especially in vessels up to 1200 tons, was only marginally, if at all, in favour of the ship. Some ships sailed better when stripped of their after-canvas, as many heavily rigged clippers griped when under full sail and required an exceptional helmsman to keep them from sailing a serpentine course: moreover a knot or two could be lost through the drag of a rudder held hard over. First class ships were often badly balanced due to wrong positioning of the masts. This defect was often corrected by removing the yards from the mizen. Most three-masted barques steered well, and this made the rig popular with the foremast hands.

The ship Torrens *in 1892*

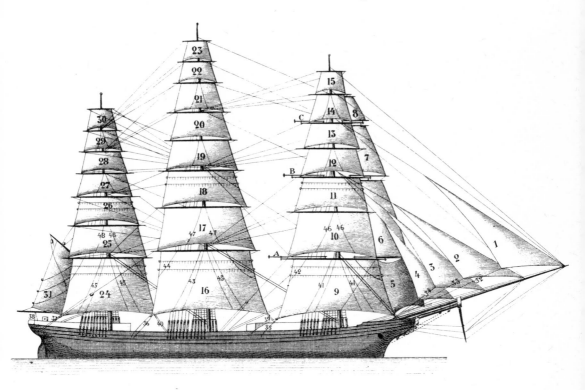

Full-rigged Ship.

1	Flying-jib.	27	Lower-mizen-topgallant-sail.
2	Outer-jib.	28	Upper-mizen-topgallant-sail.
3	Inner-jib.	29	Mizen-royal.
4	Fore-topmast-staysail.	30	Mizen-skysail.
5	Fore-lower-studding-sail	31	Spanker.
6	Fore-topmast-studding-sail.	32	Flying-jib-sheet.
7	Fore-topgallant-studding-sail.	33	Outer-jib-sheet.
8	Fore-royal-studding-sail.	34	Inner-jib-sheet.
9	Fore-sail.	35	Fore-sheet.
10	Lower-fore-topsail.	36	Main-sheet.
11	Upper-fore-topsail.	37	Crossjack-sheet.
12	Lower-fore-topgallant-sail.	38	Spanker-sheet.
13	Upper-fore-topgallant-sail.	39	Main-tack.
14	Fore-royal.	40	Crossjack-tack.
15	Fore-skysail.	41	Fore-bunt-lines.
16	Main-sail.	42	Fore-leech-line.
17	Lower-main-topsail.	43	Main-bunt-lines.
18	Upper-main-topsail.	44	Main-leech-line.
19	Lower-main-topgallant-sail.	45	Crossjack-bunt-lines.
20	Upper-main-topgallant-sail.	46	Fore-topsail-bunt-lines.
21	Main-royal.	47	Main-topsail-bunt-lines.
22	Main-skysail.	48	Mizen-topsail-bunt-lines.
23	Moonsail.	**A**	Fore-topmast-studding-sail-boom.
24	Crossjack.	**B**	Fore-topgallant-studding-sail-boom.
25	Lower-mizen-topsail.	**C**	Fore-royal-studding-sail-boom.
26	Upper-mizen-topsail.		

Ship showing Staysails, etc.

1 Flying-jib-boom.	31 Fore-royal-backstay.
2 Jib-boom.	32 Fore-skysail-backstay.
3 Bowsprit.	33 Main-staysail.
4 Martingale-boom ; Martingale.	34 Main-stay.
5 Flying-jib-boom-stay ; Flying-martingale-stay.	35 Main-topmast-staysail.
6 Jib-boom-stay ; Martingale-stay.	36 Main-topmast-stay.
7 Martingale-guys ; Martingale-back-ropes.	37 Middle-staysail.
8 Fore-skysail-stay.	38 Middle-staysail-stay.
9 Fore-royal-stay.	39 Main-topgallant-staysail.
10 Flying-jib-stay.	40 Main-topgallant-stay.
11 Fore-topgallant-stay.	41 Main-royal-staysail.
12 Jib-stay.	42 Main-royal-stay.
13 Fore-topmast-stay.	43 Main-skysail-stay.
14 Fore-stay.	44 Staysail-sheets.
15 Fore-mast.	45 Main-mast.
16 Fore-top.	46 Main-top.
17 Fore-mast-cap.	47 Main-mast-cap.
18 Fore-topmast.	48 Main-topmast.
19 Fore-topmast-crosstrees.	49 Main-topmast-crosstrees.
20 Fore-topmast-cap.	50 Main-topmast-cap.
21 Fore-topgallant-mast.	51 Main-topgallant-mast.
22 Fore-topgallant-crosstrees.	52 Main-topgallant-crosstrees.
23 Fore-topgallant-cap.	53 Main-topgallant-mast-cap.
24 Fore-royal-mast.	54 Main-royal-mast.
25 Fore-skysail-mast.	55 Main-skysail-mast.
26 Fore-skysail-pole.	56 Main-skysail-pole.
27 Fore-rigging ; Fore-lower-rigging.	57 Main-rigging ; Main-lower-rigging.
28 Fore-topmast-rigging.	58 Main-topmast-rigging.
29 Fore-topmast-backstays.	59 Main-topmast-backstays.
30 Fore-topgallant-backstays.	60 Main-topgallant-backstays.

61 Main-royal-backstay.
62 Main-skysail-backstay.
63 Mizen-staysail.
64 Mizen-stay.
65 Mizen-topmast-staysail.
66 Mizen-topmast-stay.
67 Mizen-topgallant-staysail.
68 Mizen-topgallant-stay.
69 Mizen-royal-staysail.
70 Mizen-royal-stay.
71 Mizen-skysail-stay.
72 Mizen-mast.
73 Mizen-top.
74 Mizen-mast-cap.
75 Mizen-topmast.
76 Mizen-topmast-crosstrees.
77 Mizen-topmast-cap.
78 Mizen-topgallant-mast.
79 Mizen-topgallant-crosstrees.
80 Mizen-topgallant-mast-cap.
81 Mizen-royal-mast.
82 Mizen-skysail-mast.
83 Mizen-skysail-pole.
84 Mizen-rigging ; Mizen-lower-rigging.
85 Mizen-topmast-rigging.
86 Mizen-topmast-backstays.
87 Mizen-topgallant-backstays.
88 Mizen-royal-backstay.
89 Mizen-skysail-backstay.
90 Lanyards.

Full-rigged Ship at Anchor.

1 Fore-mast.	39 Upper-mizen-topsail-yard.	74 Fore-topgallant-stay.	110 Fore-foot-rope.
2 Fore-topmast.	40 Lower-mizen-topgallant-yard.	75 Flying-jib-stay.	111 Fore-topsail-foot-ropes.
3 Fore-topgallant-mast.	41 Upper-mizen-topgallant-yard.	76 Fore-royal-stay.	112 Fore-topgallant-foot-rope.
4 Fore-royal-mast.	42 Mizen-royal-yard.	77 Fore-skysail-stay.	113 Fore-royal-foot-rope.
5 Fore-skysail-mast.	43 Mizen-skysail-yard.	78 { Flying-jib-boom-stay.	114 Fore-skysail-foot-rope.
6 Fore-skysail-pole.	44 Outriggers.	{ Flying-martingale-stay.	115 Main-foot-rope.
7 Main-mast.	45 Fore-gaff.	79 Jib-boom-stay; Martingale-stay.	116 Main-topsail-foot-ropes.
8 Main-topmast.	46 Main-gaff.	80 { Martingale-guys ;	117 Main-topgallant-foot-ropes.
9 Main-topgallant-mast.	47 Spanker-gaff.	{ Martingale-back-ropes.	118 Main-royal-foot-rope.
10 Main-royal-mast.	48 Spanker-boom.	81 Bobstays.	119 Main-skysail-foot-rope.
11 Main-skysail-mast.	49 Monkey-gaff.	82 Main-stay.	120 Crossjack-foot-rope.
12 Main-skysail-pole.	50 { Fore-rigging ;	83 Main-topmast-stay.	121 Mizen-topsail-foot-ropes.
13 Mizen-mast.	{ Fore-lower-rigging.	84 Main-topgallant-stay.	122 Mizen-topgallant-foot-rope.
14 Mizen-topmast.	51 Fore-topmast-rigging.	85 Main-royal-stay.	123 Mizen-royal-foot-rope
15 Mizen-topgallant-mast.	52 Fore-topgallant-rigging.	86 Main-skysail-stay.	124 Mizen-skysail-foot-rope.
16 Mizen-royal-mast.	53 { Main-rigging ;	87 Mizen-stay.	125 Fore-braces.
17 Mizen-skysail-mast.	{ Main-lower-rigging.	88 Mizen-topmast-stay.	126 Lower-fore-topsail-braces.
18 Mizen-skysail-pole	54 Main-topmast-rigging.	89 Mizen-topgallant-stay.	127 Upper-fore-topsail-braces.
19 Bowsprit.	55 Main-topgallant-rigging.	90 Mizen-royal-stay.	128 Lower- & Upper-fore-topgallant-
20 Jib-boom.	56 { Mizen-rigging ;	91 Mizen-skysail-stay.	braces.
21 Flying-jib-boom.	{ Mizen-lower-rigging.	92 Fore-lifts.	129 Fore-royal-brace.
22 Martingale-boom ; Martingale.	57 Mizen-topmast-rigging.	93 Fore-topgallant-lift.	130 Fore-skysail-brace.
23 Fore-yard.	58 Mizen-topgallant-rigging.	94 Fore-topgallant-lift.	131 Main-brace.
24 Lower-fore-topsail-yard.	59 Fore-topmast-backstays.	95 Fore-royal-lift.	132 Lower-main-topsail-brace.
25 Upper-fore-topsail-yard.	60 Fore-topgallant-backstays.	96 Fore-skysail-lift.	133 Upper-main-topsail-brace.
26 Lower-fore-topgallant-yard.	61 Fore-royal-backstay.	97 Main-lift.	134 Lower-main-topgallant-brace.
27 Upper-fore-topgallant-yard.	62 Fore-skysail-backstay.	98 Main-topsail-lift.	135 Upper-main-topgallant-brace.
28 Fore-royal-yard.	63 Main-topmast-backstays.	99 Main-topgallant-lift.	136 Main-royal-brace.
29 Fore-skysail-yard.	64 Main-topgallant-backstays.	100 Main-royal-lift.	137 Main-skysail-brace.
30 Main-yard.	65 Main-royal-backstay.	101 Main-skysail-lift.	138 Crossjack-brace.
31 Lower-main-topsail-yard.	66 Main-skysail-backstay.	102 Crossjack-lift.	139 Lower-mizen-topsail-brace.
32 Upper-main-topsail-yard.	67 Mizen-topmast-backstays.	103 Mizen-topsail-lift.	140 Upper-mizen-topsail-brace.
33 Lower-main-topgallant-yard.	68 Mizen-topgallant-backstays.	104 Mizen-topgallant-lift.	141 Lower-mizen-topgallant-brace.
34 Upper-main-topgallant-yard.	69 Mizen-royal-backstay.	105 Mizen-royal-lift.	142 Upper-mizen-topgallant-brace.
35 Main-royal-yard.	70 Mizen-skysail-backstay.	106 Mizen-skysail-lift.	143 Mizen-royal-brace.
36 Main-skysail-yard.	71 Fore-stay.	107 Fore-vang ; Fore-trysail-vang.	144 Mizen-skysail-braces.
37 Crossjack-yard.	72 Fore-topmast-stay.	108 Main-vang ; Main-trysail-vang.	145 Brace-pendants.
38 Lower-mizen-topsail-yard.	73 Jib-stay.	109 Spanker-vang.	

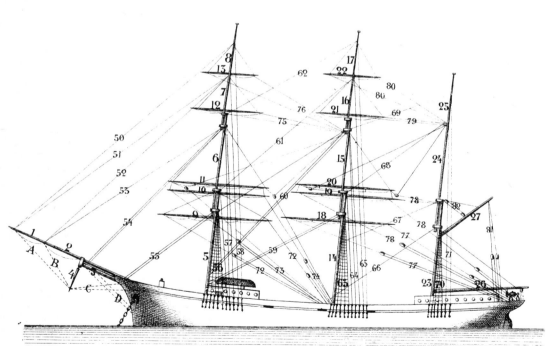

1	Flying-jib-boom.
2	Jib-boom.
3	Bowsprit.
4	Martingale-boom ; Martingale.
5	Fore-mast.
6	Fore-topmast.
7	Fore-topgallant-mast.
8	Fore-royal-mast.
9	Fore-yard.
10	Lower-fore-topsail-yard.
11	Upper-fore-topsail-yard.
12	Fore-topgallant-yard.
13	Fore-royal-yard.
14	Main-mast.
15	Main-topmast.
16	Main-topgallant-mast.
17	Main-royal-mast.
18	Main-yard.
19	Lower-main-topsail-yard.
20	Upper-main-topsail-yard.
21	Main-topgallant-yard.
22	Main-royal-yard.
23	Mizen-mast.
24	Mizen-topmast.
25	Mizen-topgallant-mast.
26	Spanker-boom.
27	Spanker-gaff.
28	Flying-jib.
29	Jib.
30	Fore-topmast-staysail.
31	Fore-sail.
32	Lower-fore-topsail.
33	Upper-fore-topsail.
34	Fore-topgallant-sail.
35	Fore-royal.
36	Main-topmast-staysail.
37	Main-middle-staysail.
38	Main-topgallant-staysail.
39	Main-royal-staysail.
40	Main-sail.
41	Lower-main-topsail.
42	Upper-main-topsail.
43	Main-topgallant-sail.
44	Main-royal.
45	Mizen-staysail.
46	Mizen-middle-staysail.
47	Mizen-topmast-staysail.
48	Spanker.
49	Gaff-topsail.
50	Fore-royal-stay.
51	Flying-jib-stay.
52	Fore-topgallant-stay.
53	Jib-stay.
54	Fore-topmast-stay.
55	Fore-stay.
56	Fore-rigging; Fore-lower-rigging.
57	Fore-topmast-backstays.
58	Fore-topgallant-, & Royal-backstays.
59	Main-stay.
60	Main-topmast-stay.
61	Main-topgallant-stay.
62	Main-royal-stay.
63	Main-rigging; Main-lower-rigging.
64	Main-topmast-backstays.
65	Main-topgallant-, & Royal-backstays.
66	Mizen-stay-
67	Mizen-middle-staysail-stay.
68	Mizen-topmast-stay.
69	Mizen-topgallant-stay.
70	Mizen-rigging ; Mizen-lower-rigging.
71	Mizen-topmast-, & Topgallant-backstays.
72	Fore-braces.
73 74	Lower-, & Upper-fore-topsail-braces.
75	Fore-topgallant-braces.
76	Fore-royal-braces.
77	Main-braces.
78	Lower-, & Upper-main-topsail-braces.
79	Main-topgallant-braces.
80	Main-royal-braces.
81	Spanker-vangs.
82	Spanker-peak-fall.
83	Fore-bunt-lines.
84	Fore-leech-lines.
85	Main-bunt-lines.
86	Main-leech-line.
A	Flying-jib-boom-stay. Flying-martingale-stay.
B	Jib-boom-stay ; Martingale-stay.
C	Martingale-guys ; Martingale-back-ropes.
D	Bobstays.

APPENDIX B

Principal Ships Mentioned

The following details of the *Caroline*, the *Orpheus*, the *Vanguard* and the *Orient* are extracted from *Lloyd's Registry of Shipping:*

Caroline
Built at Quebec in 1828, 425 tons, for Atkinson; of white oak, sheathed with yellow metal and copper-fastened registered in London and A1 at Lloyd's (8 years).

In 1828 she was rigged as a ship, with W. Kent as master, on the route from London to Quebec. From 1829 to 1838 she traded on the same route, although under the ownership of J. Allan and with J. Greig as master. From 1836 onwards she was barque-rigged (see Appendix A). In 1839, with Anderson as master, she made a voyage from London to Sydney, then reverted to the Quebec route until her disappearance from the register in 1845.

Orpheus
Built at New York in 1832, 573 tons, for N. Cobb; of white oak and pitch pine, sheathed with copper; registered in New York, trading between that port and Liverpool.

She was not recorded in the register for 1834, when C. H. Clarke sailed in her, but according to Lloyd's records was still sailing between New York and Liverpool in 1839 under the command of Captain Bursley.

There are several references to the *Orpheus* and to Captain Bursley in *Square-Riggers on Schedule* by Robert Greenhalgh (Princeton University Press, 1938), which contains the following information: '*Orpheus* built at New York by C. Bergh & Co. in 1833, length 132 ft, depth of hold 15 ft 6 in. Line service began 1834, ended 1839.'

The *Orpheus* mentioned by Carl C. Cutler in *Greyhounds of the Sea* (published by G. P. Putnam's Sons) as sailing from New York to San Francisco in 1849 on a passage of 159 days, was probably a different vessel. In either case the ultimate fate of the ship is not known.

Vanguard
Built at Sunderland in 1857, 626 tons, for J. Kelso, of wood sheathed with yellow metal and copper-fastened; registered in Shields.

She was initially rigged as a ship and from 1857 to 1865 traded for Kelso under the command of Scott on the China route. In 1866 and 1867 she was engaged in coastal and continental trading; in 1868 she was converted to barque rig and in that and the following year again sailed to China with T. Hunter as master. In 1870 she was sold to John Baker of London and was extensively altered, seven feet being added to her original length of 154 ft: she traded on the coast and to the continent for three years under the command of J. Green. I. R. Luckiss became her master in 1873, sailing to Japan in that year and then to coastal and continental ports in 1875 and 1876. In the two years following she continued in the same trade under W. S. Watts and W. Boniface, but disappeared from the register in 1878. In the records for 1874 there is a note 'damage repaired'.